Choking On Silence

By PAUL B. TRIPP

Aly —
Many This Jorney inspire
you of the work you
do on behalf of the
Many. Best —

This memoir is based upon my experiences over a forty year period. Names have been changed, locations switched, and events compressed

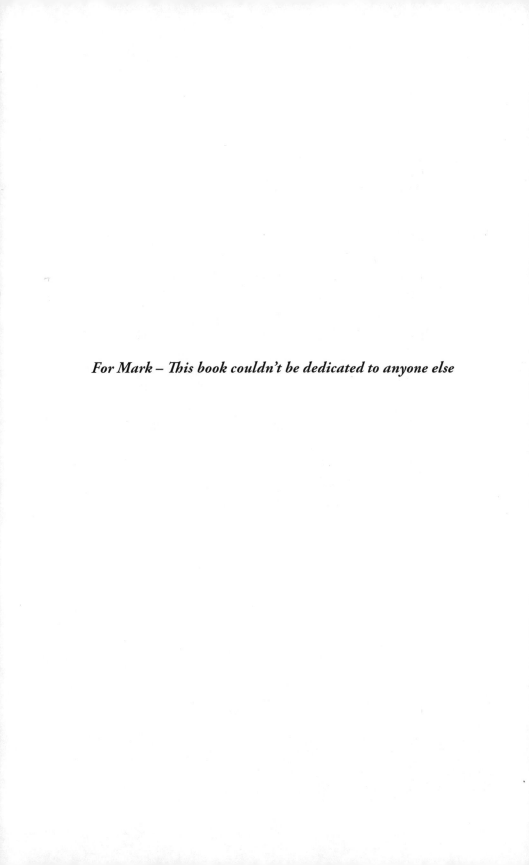

For Mark – This book couldn't be dedicated to anyone else

ACKNOWLEDGMENTS

Teri Allen – *"Commander"* – Your gracious offer to edit my book was a gift I didn't know I needed until I saw your wisdom carve breath into my story. Although I can't promise I will tattoo your name to my forehead, I am seriously considering it.

Charles Warren New York – *"Parsons"* – The friend I never expected to have, and a man who was born knowing who he is. Your gentle whispers helped me find my way.

Bruce and Nancy Bugbee – A long stretch of Montana highway is where I believe our friendship was cemented. Thank you for your candor, your encouragement and the "notes."

Dave McKean – *Service Legal Defense Network* – Your legal guidance was a key component in allowing me to feel comfortable enough to tell my story. Thank you for your continued work defending and empowering LGBT service members, veterans and their families.

Kris Hermanns – *Pride Foundation Executive Director* – I am impressed with your leadership, vision and passion for LGBT issues. I look forward to a lasting partnership with the Pride Foundation.

FOREWORD

For as long as I can remember I have looked at the gay lifestyle as if it belonged to someone else. A young man from Montana, who accepted Christ at an early age, joined the military and believed in reparative therapy for homosexuality – I've always tried to pretend I was just like every other heterosexual male – until I closed the bedroom door.

Some of you might think that you've read this story before – but you haven't – because I didn't know this story existed until two years ago. I was at work crunching financial numbers when I heard the still voice of the Holy Spirit speak directly in my ears. It was only the second time in my life I have heard this still voice, and I was the kid who spent the first thirteen years of my life not believing in God. Is it possible for a homosexual to hear the voice of God? Apparently the answer is yes because I quit my job that very day and for the next three months I did nothing but paint the inside of my house, and pray, which is how this book was born.

Although I have felt the stirrings of a book for quite some time, it was the combination of Jesus Christ, the repeal of "Don't Ask, Don't Tell" and a request from the Pride Foundation that created a perfect "creative" storm within my life. Shy and private, writing a book about my most intimate moments was unfathomable, and yet here it is.

There's a lot of story on the next few hundred pages, forty-four years to be exact. I didn't write this book in order and I didn't write it for any particular audience, as I believe the human struggle is germane to all of us. Forced to classify my memoir into a category, I cringed when I had to select "Gay and Lesbian" issues, for that's just a small part of how I understand myself. While homosexuality serves as the underpinning for this book, I believe life's lessons apply equally across the board. The confusion of religion, our awkward twenties, the dance of finding a mate and the stressors of our careers; we all relate to one another beyond whom we choose to sleep with in the bedroom.

With that disclaimer aside, I want to address the teenage suicides that have swept across our great country the past few years. Newscasters have tagged these suicides as sexual confusion, school bullying and difficult home lives. Oddly enough, I can relate to all three. Adolescent pain -- sucks – plain and simple. The flip side to that coin is that pain is an opportunity for growth, and that's the message I want to communicate to all of the teenagers and young adults reading my book. Although I have thought about, made several plans and longed to end my life on the darkest of days – I always knew in my heart that I wanted my life to stand for something other than "he killed himself." I never knew the answers to my life when I was living it in the present – all I had was a determination and a faith that if I believed in my actions strongly enough, my life would work itself out. As you read my book, please remember that I understand and I hope that my words will encourage you to choose a living solution to your short-term problem, rather than the permanent option I understand so well. I hope that by the time you're done reading this you will believe that you can be the person who defies your uncomfortable circumstances and rises above them to achieve beyond what anyone thought possible.

To the parents of gay children - I hope this story illuminates an understanding that you didn't know existed. Religion and talking heads aside, it's your turn to think critically about your child's struggles in an attempt to understand their lives. As you are aware, parental acceptance can either be a major boost or a monumental hurdle in your child's ability to succeed in this world. My greatest desire is that by reading my journey you will see your children through new eyes and experience a love for them as the day you saw them for the very first time.

My military brothers and sisters never asked for homosexuality to be brought front and center into their work lives. I suppose if we were to rewind the clock several decades, the same thing could have been said when blacks and women were integrated into the military. Sometimes a silence needs to be broken so that healing can occur, and I hope my story is a first step in our collective understanding of just how aggressively the military discriminated against homosexuals who desired to serve. My story isn't intended to disrespect the cause for which we stand or the service we provide to this great Country. As military members we are charged with conducting ourselves in the most professional manner possible while doing the right thing in the face of adversity and quite possibility, a hefty amount of criticism. I have no doubt criticism will come; however, as I weather the withering tongues, I hope you will welcome your gay brothers and sisters with as much acceptance as everyone else with whom you serve alongside

There isn't enough money on earth nor a guarantee of anything – including health – that would make me sacrifice my current life to go back and live as a married homosexual male living in a heterosexual world and struggling through reparative therapy and the shame surrounding religion. Is homosexuality a sin? Is it possible to be a gay Christian? I think my perspective is going to surprise you.

I hope the following pages piss you off and inspire you – all in the same moment. It's a true story and I stand at attention behind every single keystroke even though I'm now retired from the military. God, submarines, homosexuality, the National Security Agency, reparative therapy, marriage, what it means to love a person who is HIV positive….and well, you'll have to read about the rest.

I hope this story touches your heart as much as it has touched mine.

PART ONE

BEGINNINGS

As I came through the door, my bloody nose turning the shag carpet crimson red, my stepmother Lynn told me to take a deep breath and start from the beginning. The beginning — it's always the hardest place to start.

I grew up on a dirt road which was oiled as regularly as my dad oiled his thirst for booze, women and money. Slicked back light brown hair, piercing green eyes, meaty hands that worked on the ends of beefy forearms, six tattoos, six kids in his family, manicured fingernails and cardigan sweaters — nobody dared to call my dad a faggot. He drove a big eighteen wheeler through the mud, snow and dirt wearing a tucked-in shirt, polished shoes and a belt to match. A ladies man through and through, if he wasn't flirting he was fighting, and in my little town of Missoula, Montana my father had a reputation for beating up the homos. My grandma Maxine was one of the few women who thought my dad was a time bomb, and who stopped talking to my parents for one year after they eloped. Getting hitched was supposed to happen in the church, but instead my dad hitched up a trailer and my mom to his truck and away they went to Idaho to say "I Do." Of course it was the reason you suspect; bad boy meets good girl always equals a demon child.

Holly, she's the demon child, the bane of my childhood existence. Just sixteen months older -- old enough to beat the crap out of me until I hit my teenage years -- she was the first person to teach me the injustices of life. Holly took after my father; a tank with strong hands, thick legs and bushy eyebrows. Even when we played doctor, we fought. Holly had to have everything her way; she was the patient, doctor, nurse, nurse manager, physical therapist, front desk clerk and parking attendant. It was always my job to process the insurance forms, in silence. In Holly's eyes, I was her puppet and she was my master. It was a theme that played itself down the middle of our childhood, ripping us apart like the paper seal from a whiskey bottle. A daddy's girl, she took to the booze like a fish takes to water, while I remained on land. Diving out to sea, she disappeared from view after she left home and I haven't seen her since.

My mom was never a drinker; she just turned mean for the fifteen years after my father broke her nose. Standing a steady 5'5", size two and hair taller than the width of her waist, she had higher hopes than we did on receiving the perfect mother of the year award. She never received that fateful call to come and claim her award, and it's probably just as well because her marriage had twisted so many of her limbs she wouldn't have had the energy to walk up on the stage. A good Catholic girl who left Montana to join a convent, she came home right before she took her holy vows, and my father knocked the holiness right out of her, leaving a hole in her heart which she stuffed with bloody rags until we left home.

Me? Well, I was born in a big city but somehow came out of my mother's womb in Montana, and like a trout swimming upstream to spawn, I was biologically wired to leave and achieve. I suppose my mom's bedtime rule tells you almost everything you need to know about me. Whatever time I got out of bed in the morning, was the same time I had to go to bed at night. I thought 4:00 a.m. was a reasonable time to greet the neighbors until my mom closed the blinds at 3:59 p.m. and pulled my bed covers back. With blond hair, bedroom eyes and a pot belly, I had more energy than a Mexican jumping bean. I quickly identified my talent of fifty questions, singing, eating dessert and dancing –- all in that order. By the fourth grade I was as quick as lightning and had mastered counseling for traumatic stress, pill taking (for an ulcer) and had already been on a diet, showing the first signs of my overachieving abilities. Unless you call "faggot," "queer," "gay" and "stupid" popular terms, I wasn't popular.

I don't want to give you the wrong impression here; this isn't going to be one of those stories of a broken home and victorious victim. I've never seen myself as a victim. I was just a kid who got put on a bucking bronco well before I learned how to spell horse, bull or bullshit, but I held on for the ride because I can't stand not coming in first place. You see, you don't have to be "proclaimed" to know you are a winner. What you have to do, however, is lead an authentic life.

TEENAGE GROWTH

(Ages 10-14)

In 1979, Missoula was a town that believed academia was for the east coast, singing for the west coast and the white jeans that I wore on the first day of sixth grade were only supposed to be seen in fashion magazines. Sixth grade, I should have never started. When Ellen interviews me for this book and asks what I want to tell my toddler self, I'm going to tell him to skip immediately to the summer of my eighth grade year.

Sixth grade was the year before we got a shopping mall and I discovered that brown shoes with big brown laces were no longer in style. I started that year living with my dad after my parents got divorced, attending Lewis and Clark grade school, the place where my troubles began outside of the house. I suppose I shouldn't have raised my hand to ask why Lewis got to say his name first because alphabetically C was before L, and we always had to line up in name order. Clearly focused on east coast academia, my question floated in the air like a fart in church and it didn't take long for the other sixth graders to discover I was different and assume a pack mentality against me. Kristy, Kim and Tina were the wolves who ate my spirit, lunch and all possible friendships for the next three years.

Today we call these ladies bullies, but back then I just called them bitches. There wasn't a teacher, counselor or adult in the schools who had any desire to understand the effects of bullying, and in 1979 young men were classified as either boys or sissies. Montana is where tough men are raised, not scholars, singers or fashion designers. It was the land of the free and the home of the brave, good ole M-O-N-T-A-N-A. The boys in my school had aspirations of logging, trucking and fighting forest fires. Since I went home to a forest fire every night and put on my firefighting equipment as soon as I got off of the school bus, I had aspirations of becoming a famous ballet dancer in New York. Tight legs, expressive arms, music floating all around me while I showed the world true beauty; I had visions of a trucker from Montana delivering all of the furniture to my ultra-chic Greenwich Village apartment. I could see myself greeting him at the door with sunglasses, a scarf and a $5 tip. I would tell him exactly where to put things. With my body in Missoula and my mind in the clouds, it was just a matter of time before I gained enough courage to float away.

Kristy was the biggest bully of the bunch. She was a tall gangly blond with a forked tongue, half-moon eyebrows, extended eyelashes and soulless eyes. Kristy was as cute as a Barbie and as venomous as a snake. I could smell evil reeking from her pores when she smiled at me and doled out pain. It was a sickly-sweet smirk that kept the teachers fooled, the boys swooning, and me, terrified of what she would do next. Faggot, fag, pussy, asshole, fucking moron, queer and gay boy — she had a vocabulary as big as her two front teeth. With breasts as ripe as melons, she held a spell over David and John, the two biggest bullies in our school. They'd beat me up on her command. It just took one of her magic blinks and coy little smiles and David would be over at my desk pounding his fist into his hand, warning me that not even the long yellow school bus could save me from my fate. Day after blessed day, Kristy made sure I said my prayers morning, noon and night. There wasn't a day that went by I didn't wish she could be folded up and put away like my failing math homework. My step mom Lynn use to fold up notes and stuff them into my lunch bag providing me with words of wisdom, but unfortunately her words fell flat as David pounded his fist into his flat palm. In 1979, Columbine wasn't part of our collective psyche yet, although Kristy routinely pushed me towards thoughts of unforgiving pain. I can still feel her knocking the breath out of me thirty-two years later.

Kim and Tina were the brawn behind Kristy's brains. Brown haired minus the beauty, these two survived by following the pack, tearing the backpack off my back and shoving me to the ground or into my desk as frequently as they could. Manipulative little monsters, they pretended to be my friends when Kristy wasn't around, and then threw me in the trash as soon as miss long lashes sauntered back into the room. They weren't popular enough to organize a full blown coup to have me killed outright, but they wielded just enough power to keep me crippled in academics and gym class.

Tired of the bullying and the faggot label that had been sewn into my back since the sixth grade, I proclaimed to my parents that I was going to move out of Montana and become a foreign exchange student. My dad wanted to know who in the hell was going to pay for it and reminded me that he sure as hell didn't have that kind of money. In his defense, alcohol was really expensive back then. When I told my mom, she just looked at me as if I had told her I had AIDS. A blank stare, nothing more — the same look she gave me when she told me I had to get an HIV test if I wanted to live in her house again. Oh yeah, I got the test my senior year of high school and then moved out as quickly as I had moved in, but I don't want to get too far ahead of my story, so let's get back to the summer my life turned on a dime.

The summer before I started high school I moved back in with my mom. With the lectures from my father six miles away, I had nothing but a delicious summer stretched out before me like a yellow Slip and Slide. Within the first week, my mother stated she was not content to have me sit around the house and decided I needed a good summer project to keep me busy. As luck would have it, she had been looking for quite some time and signed me up to work at a nursing home as a volunteer coordinator where I would get to ride my bike along the busy street twice a day and work for free. Perfect.

A halfway suicidal pubescent teenager with rage so strong I could have starred as the Incredible Hulk, the local nursing home sounded like a perfect fit! The youngest volunteer on record, I organized games, pushed old people to lunch and handed out ice cream — as much as I could fit on top of a cone. Unable to kill myself, I served up Dr. Kevorkian portions to clog the arteries of everyone with Alzheimer's and dementia. Those old people loved it when I came wheeling around the corner with my portable ice cream killing machine.

Dorothy loved ice cream, ah yes good ole Dorothy, she was my favorite. Dorothy was a regal old woman with stark white hair, polished shoes, elegant jewelry, a shawl around her shoulders, a blanket on her lap and her Foley catheter bag hanging off the back of her wheelchair like a pair of fuzzy dice on a rearview mirror. I'm convinced that Dorothy was a stage performer, which is how she caught my attention. The diva of the nursing home, Frank Sinatra was her man of choice. Dorothy sang about my melancholy life and my future dreams all wrapped up into a tight ball of

Kleenex, which she kept tucked in the left sleeve of her blouse. If I wasn't doling out ice cream, Dorothy and I were on the dole, careening around that dimly-lit prison full of nothing but memories. With the promises of hope spent in their youth, the inhabitants had nothing but death awaiting them, and of course, a song from Dorothy. She knew every lyric to every song, but had to ask me who in the hell I was day after song-filled day. I was the stranger who came into her life each morning and left every afternoon. She was always so surprised to see me, like a bird looking up from the grass just as it puts a worm into its mouth. She'd belt out a song and off we'd go with me pushing from behind. She knew she didn't belong there, and neither did I. I was stuck there for a summer and she, for the rest of her life. I was the only visitor knocking on Dorothy's door, until she answered death's knock two years later.

The nursing home was the first place I felt acceptance. I was a hyperactive child, a brother who couldn't do anything right, a kid who was labeled as a faggot at school, a child of an active alcoholic and the product of a bitter divorce. In 1979, there were no stories to convince me that life gets better; no way for me to know that it was normal for teenagers to struggle with their sexual identity; no school policies to prevent bullying. I felt like the lone sailboat in a regatta whose ship had capsized and been forgotten. The monstrous waves of my home life and elementary school experiences caused me to gasp for breath as I managed to keep my head just above the waterline, wondering if taking my own life wasn't a better choice. Hopeless, alone and struggling to understand my place in the world, the nursing home brought me a sense of purpose. It was the only place I believed I was making a difference, a place of acceptance and love.

JESUS CHRIST

(Age 14)

I had been contemplating suicide for most of my childhood until the summer I met Pastor Steve Valentine. It was the same summer I began screwing around with the neighborhood boys; the first summer I mentally acknowledged my homosexuality.

Kim King, the volunteer coordinator at the nursing home, had invited me up to a BBQ in Pattee Canyon organized by the Clark Fork Christian Center Youth Group and Church. A woman on the shorter side of life, Kim had brown hair, a brown Toyota and brown eyes. She took a liking to me my first day on the job at the nursing home by assigning me to the ice cream cart. She never mentioned the joy ice cream brings to nursing home patients, nor did she ever mention the joy of Jesus Christ. Instead, she invited me to head up and play some volleyball and with nothing but my empty bedroom waiting for me at home, I decided to go.

Besides the Sunday mornings when I tried to avoid going to the Catholic Church with my mother, I hadn't ever really thought about God. I didn't know anything about being born again other than the fantasies of wanting a new family. Church had always made me sleepy. Bless this, bless that, kneel, stand, pray and then kneel some more — none of it made any sense. I had enough rituals at home with my assigned chores; I certainly didn't feel any desire to give up more of my free time to a God who seemed further away than my own thoughts. Religion in my house was defined as my father's alcohol bottle, my mother's tears and my sister's empty accusations of my guilt.

Hot dogs, hamburgers, Diet Coke and laughter — that's what led me to Christ. I was showered with acceptance as I missed the volleyball, tripped over my own shoe laces and talked to a woman only to discover later that I had ketchup stuck in the corners of my mouth. This group of people didn't care about what the kids at school thought about me, what my parents did for a living, or what kind of beverage my father liked. It was the first time in my young life that I wasn't forced to explain the sins of my family or why I deserved the bullying at school. I felt free . . . absolutely free.

Towards the end of the day Pastor Valentine gathered us up into a group; we grasped hands, bowed our heads and prayed. I remember him thanking God for the beautiful weather, the fellowship of the Youth Group and then, he thanked the Lord for me. He thanked God for guiding me to the BBQ. Me, Paul . . . he thanked God for me. He thanked God. For. Me. I had managed to lose the volleyball game for my team and not wipe my mouth off properly, and he was thanking me for coming. When Pastor Valentine asked if there was anyone in the group who would like to accept Jesus Christ as their personal Lord and Savior, my tear-stained cheeks and I stepped forward into the circle. Standing in the center of attention, the entire group put their hands on me as Pastor Valentine and I recited the prayer together. People were mumbling thanks, Pastor Valentine was praying a blessing over my life, and I was in the center crying. In that singular moment, I felt the sweetness of the Holy Spirit swoop down from heaven above and wipe my spirit free of pain. I truly felt born again.

Within a week I was attending church at the Clark Fork Christian Center on a regular basis and had joined the Youth Group. Two weeks later I was anointed with the gift of praying in tongues. Seated in Pastor Valentine's office, my private prayer language came spewing out of my mouth before I knew what was happening. I had never heard of anyone praying in anything other than English so when I started speaking in tongues it scared me half to death. A prayer language from my heart to God's ears; that's what Pastor Valentine told me. He said I was allowed to pray in tongues anytime I felt led by the Holy Spirit to do so, which is exactly what I did.

By the end of the summer of my eighth grade year I was praying all day long and had been baptized in a swimming pool at one of the local hotels. I was an active member of the Youth Group, reading my Bible several hours a day and was attending church for several hours on Sunday morning. The sweetness of standing in the prayer room with the sun beaming in through the windows with my hands lifted to Christ, praying in tongues and singing is how my summer ended. Anointed as a new child of God, I was ready to start high school.

Big Sky High School was plopped in the middle of a muddy field, just across from my house. With the bullies Kristy and Tina at the rival school across town, and I newly baptized and slain in the Holy Spirit, my freshmen year promised nothing but minty freshness. A new school and God planted firmly in my right front pocket, I believed His words and walked into high school cleansed of all of my sins. Football, cheerleading and basketball were the flavors of the year, so I chose choir instead. Music and God were my saving grace those first two years. A devout homosexual teenage Christian; lotion and my Bible sat right next to one another, each one promising to bring me happiness in unspeakable ways.

After a few months of high school I confessed my secret to Pastor Valentine, who promptly told me of my sins. Not only was I not allowed to touch another boy's penis, I wasn't allowed to touch my own, and it was made abundantly clear that if I kissed a girl I was committing adultery because I was kissing another man's future wife. I think I lasted three weeks, far short of the forty days and forty nights Pastor Valentine prescribed, before I had an explosion and then another, and another. That was the beginning of my contradiction –- a young man with homosexual desires trying to live a holy life. A hole in my heart from a wretched home-life, a school environment full of mediocrity, and without one friend with whom I could relate, I made good on my promise and moved to South America.

SOUTH AMERICA TO LOS ANGELES

(Ages 16 – 18)

Before I got off of the airplane in South America, I unzipped myself from Montana, unpacked the new person I had hidden away in my suitcase and stepped into my new skin. I had a lot of baggage for a sixteen-year-old, but besides my red Michael Jackson jacket, brown boots and hydrogen peroxide bleached hair, the only other things I brought with me were God and homosexuality. Pastor Valentine had made it abundantly clear that homosexuality and God worked in opposition to each other. Unsure of just how right he was, I attempted to be honest to both while being dishonest with myself. I was hoping my year in South America would provide me with some answers.

It took me about three months to unravel the gibber and the jabber of the Spanish language. Without any classroom guidance on how to conjugate verbs, I learned through listening, which is how my American parents taught me fear, anger and abandonment. Determined to break the cycle of madness, I worked to feel love for my host family and the boys at school helped in that process by showing endless curiosity towards me. My teenage years were finally free from daily sexual questioning and I basked in the sunlight of new experiences which distracted my mind 24/7. With no girls in my life except my host mother, I couldn't have been happier.

I hit my stride around the fourth month, hanging out with my classmates after school smoking cigarettes, playing soccer, dancing salsa and drinking Colombian coffee. I celebrated by allowing myself to venture further and further out from the house alone. I became accustomed to taking the bus downtown or up to Unicentro, the biggest shopping mall in Bogota. I forgot that I had blond hair and blue/green bedroom eyes, and truly began to feel as if my skin had somehow changed to brown, along with every other part of my body.

Just like when I accepted Christ, Bogota shifted the tectonic plates of my life. I felt a new sense of importance as I mastered the Spanish language, my school work and worked my way into the heart of my host family. Becoming an exchange student had validated my person and provided me a living example that I could indeed become whomever I wanted, as long as I was willing to face my fears and push forward.

I'd thought that Latin culture and God were as tight as the rosary in the Pope's hand, but in the four months since my arrival we hadn't so much as graced the steps of a single church. No prayers before dinner and no longing cries to be blessed, bless others or even a God bless when they sneezed. God had clearly been painted out of the scenery of this family's life. I was too busy trying to be master of my new domain to give God much thought, and I certainly wasn't going to ask to go to church outside of school. I was more focused on blowing my train's steam whistle at night so I could focus during the day, rather than focus on His word and wait for an answer. Bogota was the first place and time I put myself before everything else, a luxury my life in Montana did not allow, and God was no exception.

The only obstacle in my Colombian life was my host brother, Carlos, who continued to push back against any form of acceptance my host family attempted to give me. Much to my surprise, my host mom and dad arranged to take the entire family, Carlos and I included, on a vacation through the coffee-filled landscape of Colombia, ending up on the coast of Santa Marta. It was there I watched a woman drown, the waves sucking her out to sea as her husband and children screamed from the beach. The ocean brought back her lifeless body, and I'll never forget the memory of that nightmarish day. It was the first time I witnessed the brutality of sudden death and as quick as a folding wave, my host mother ordered us to fold up our clothes and leave. We drove to Cartagena that same afternoon.

All the way to Cartagena, Carlos had been bantering back and forth with me, and his behavior was starting to grate on my nerves. I knew enough Spanish at this point to understand the difference between sarcasm and a pointed jab, and it became clear to me that his intent was to invite me to joust with him until one of us died a quick death. I had prepared myself for this battle before we left Bogota, speaking with Carlos' best friend about their time together in Miami. It was a conversation that fortuitously dropped into my lap without so much as a single prompt from me, and one I had filed away for future use. According to his friend's wagging tongue, Carlos had declared his sexual — homosexual — freedom in the gay bars and beaches of Miami the year prior, a fact which left his best friend befuddled. You see, Carlos was due to get married within the year.

Carlos' fiancé had been nothing but kind to me, and at the tender age of sixteen I was fully aware of the hellish contradictions homosexual feelings can cause. I knew that speaking the truth of what I had heard to my host family would be considered a direct attack on the family's honor, not to mention Carlos himself. While I didn't want to inflict damage, I had gained enough self-respect to know that I wasn't going to tolerate any more bullying in my life. Carlos was a bully, and as a guest in his home, I believed I had no other choice but to speak up and face my attacker eye-to-eye. As we hiked through the castle of old ruins, my trump card tucked safely in my breast pocket, I waited until Carlos and I were completely alone to confront him. In my best Spanish possible I called him out on his behavior and asked him to please welcome me into his home as his parents had. Infuriated, he lashed back, and it was then that I spilled the beans that I knew he liked tube steak better than fish, and if he wanted to keep it a secret he had better act like a human being towards me. That was the start of my "brutal honesty" approach to life, the day I decided to become a man and stand on my own two feet to defend my honor. Brutal honesty — it remains my greatest strength and most vulnerable weakness.

Before I could say Salto De Tecendama, a cascading waterfall right outside of Bogota, he approached my host parents in a closed-door meeting and told them that I had come to him expressing a crush, made a sexual advance and stated I am gay. My brutal honesty about his situation, not mine, had exposed my underbelly and he took advantage of my attempted blackmail by cutting me open from ear to toe. With his truth exposed, risking his engagement to a woman who had no idea of his desires, he insisted I be kicked out of their home immediately and sent back to America. It was my first encounter with a man who was to be married, but longing for a life outside of himself. Unfortunately, my words cut too close to his secret, and I paid the price as we sat down to dinner that night.

I always saw the anger in my American father's eyes before he exploded in rage, so when my host mother had the same pinched look on her face at dinner I knew something was wrong. The family closed ranks and the three-day car trip back to Bogota was met in silence. Not knowing what had transpired, I kept digging and digging and asking and asking and not a word was said until the night we arrived back home and the Exchange Student Coordinator was waiting for us in the driveway. No family meeting to talk about what had happened, I was asked to pack my bags and get in the coordinator's car. As we sped away she began screaming at the top of her lungs about my ungratefulness and my host brother's statement that I'd supposedly confessed my homosexual desires. Like Peter in the Bible, that was the first time I denied my sexual orientation to an adult who asked me directly — a pattern I would repeat for the next 15 years. Crowing like a rooster, I vehemently denied any desire towards the same sex and stated I had no idea what she was talking about. Amid a cacophony of shrills and silence, I moved in with the coordinator, my fate in her hands. I never saw my first host family again.

The irony of this situation was not lost on me, and I feared that God was somehow punishing me for my unresolved homosexual desires. I had not — absolutely 100% not — expressed any attraction, made an advance or told Carlos that I was also struggling with homosexual desires. I had been grateful that the language and culture had been so demanding on me, for it gave me a reprieve from my sexual conundrum with God. I had no intention of coming out to anyone in Bogota, all I wanted was for Carlos to treat me as a member of the family instead of some intruder who had invaded his life. Hosting an exchange student is probably a major pain in the ass, but when the parents signed up to house me, so did both host brothers. Unsteady on my feet, I had used a brutally honest approach that had somehow tapped into all of the unresolved anger I felt as a child, and I had been kicked out of my host family's house for it. That was the first time since had arrived in Bogota that I got out my Bible and prayed.

In a state of limbo, I was forced to live with the Exchange Student Coordinator for several weeks. She screamed about homosexuality, channeling my father's lecturing voice minus the booze-slurred words every chance she got. A sin, a violation of God, a pitiful and dangerous life, the worst kind of human being — I heard it all, and remained absolutely silent about my same-sex attractions. She spoke the same words as Pastor Valentine but with less finesse and a lot more judgment. While I had felt guilty when I got an erection looking at another man, she made me feel downright dirty. She crossed the line between an expression of distaste and a fiery condemnation sermon that homosexuals were an abomination of God. The

Exchange Student Coordinator's house is where I learned to shed tears of shame around feelings I could not control.

After weeks of her verbal torment, she found a young man who expressed interest in hosting me. Julio Cesar — the most unpopular kid in school. A young man who spoke with a lisp, had hands like a T-Rex and parents wealthier than Richie Rich, he was the only person who stepped up to take me in. It still embarrasses me to admit that I viewed his act of kindness as a way to boost his popularity instead of actually caring about me. But it's the truth.

Julio Cesar's family lived in a house in the northern part of Bogota — a six-story, six-car-garage monstrosity of a home. There were three live-in maids, a waterfall that fell from the sixth to the first floor and sparkling chandeliers in almost every room. I had my own bedroom, bathroom and young maid to pick up after me. This family had three homes. I had three new host brothers, one new host sister and a host mother and father who had more heart than even the biggest emeralds dangling from my host mother's ears and fingers. They owned several large bathroom supply stores throughout Bogota, and each child, with the exception of Julio Cesar, was given their own store. My new family worked, didn't go to church and traveled with suitcases of cash and guns in every car. I knew they meant business.

While the luxuries around me increased, my personal freedom decreased. I wasn't allowed to leave the house by myself, and my friends at school weren't allowed to come over unless I asked permission. I was now straddling a new socioeconomic structure and it was made subtly clear that my personal affiliations had to be approved, monitored and regulated. School stayed the same and, as expected, Julio Cesar's standing grew to over six feet tall. The family showered me with love and I became their token American son whom they paraded out at every social event possible.

Stoic and reserved, my second host family was nothing if not gracious and worked hard to accept me into their home, especially after the Exchange Student Coordinator told them of what she understood to be my "situation." My first host brother a distant memory, I kept my mouth shut about everyone and everything and just focused on my school work and my male friends, heading to strip clubs and dance joints whenever possible. Of course I brought Julio Cesar along, for he was the carrier pigeon who would eventually bring news back home that I was indeed as straight as they come. Since I knew there wasn't a chance I would be allowed to leave the house alone, sex with a woman was out of the question, so I flirted and flounced unabashedly. By the time I got on the plane to fly back to America my host parents lamented that I couldn't actually marry the young lady I had been allowed to see. She was a nice young lady, but I knew I wasn't capable of taking a wife while wanting a husband.

Back in America and tasked with completing my senior year of high school, I was restless, bored and underwhelmed by the Montana culture once again. I was no longer the fair-haired American who was revered for his language abilities, love of food or rhythmic acumen on the dance floor. My days of salsa dancing, smoking in the boy's room and tours of Unicentro –– the finest shopping mall in Bogota where a hot piece of French bread awaited me daily –– were over. I was once again a Tripp, suffocating in the small town mindset of underachievement and homophobia. Two months back home I moved out of both of my parent's homes, got an apartment, a job washing dishes and decided I would create my own fun.

Alone in an apartment with a futon, two chairs, a job and the slog of high school, by the time December 1985 rolled around I was heading in a dangerous direction. Danger knocked on my door in the form of a married guy upstairs, the local UPS driver, who wanted to deliver personal packages when his wife wasn't home. He was a rapid reminder of Carlos in Bogota and I shut the door on him, and quick. Then there was the guy I met at a bar who came over one night and left my oven on while I was asleep because I wouldn't give him sex. My conundrum of wanting some type of intimate connection with a man, besides just sex, had begun.

In April 1986 shortly after my eighteenth birthday, I got on a plane bound for Hawaii and was determined to never come back. It wasn't an intentional move on my part as I really was heading over there for spring break, but one day led to two days and before I knew it I was finishing high school through a correspondence course and informed my family to send me my things. I met some locals and before the last night of my vacation finished I was hauling my luggage out of the hotel and into a two- bedroom apartment that was housing eight other people. A living room floor with a view and a soft fluffy pillow, I lived in that apartment for two months.

Hawaii was another turning point in my psyche. I began to realize the power of being a young gay man working in a gay restaurant where youth was revered. Youth was, and probably still is, the premier calling card for most gay men and coming from Montana I had a side of innocence that was attractive to anyone looking for a main course. I could have given in and become a house boy to a rich Canadian, a hunk from Italy or an aging man from Colorado. Offer after offer, I learned that even older men are lonely — not just eighteen year olds — and for some reason I knew better than to throw away my youth just to satisfy the desire of an older man.

Like every tourist in Hawaii, I believed true love would come my way, and with the home court advantage of actually living in Hawaii, I thought love was only a matter of time. White Midwesterners, honeymooning Japanese, and couples with children traipsed in and out of the local hotels like a revolving door. Week after week I stood and greeted the gay men who were there on vacation from all over the world. Most stayed long enough for me to capture their life stories, but not long enough to create one of our own. Faced with copious offers for one-night stands, the invitations lost their allure shortly after I arrived. Instead, I walked the beach in the early mornings, took naps in the afternoons and worked the evening shifts, flirting unabashedly for tips. By my second month in Honolulu I realized I had made a mistake. True love wasn't coming by ship, or by plane.

Enter Tom from Los Angeles. I was the host with the most the day he walked into my life. To me he was just another hot guy from the mainland wanting a good time in Hawaii and I was not amused. He was there with his friend, who had just found out he was HIV positive and heading towards the last turnstile on his final ride home. As an eighteen-year-old with the cautious perspective of an eighty- year-old I couldn't be bothered. But Tom kept coming back and coming back and coming back to Honolulu. By his third trip, I knew he was serious. He asked me to move to Los Angeles and live with him. We both knew it wasn't love, but I wondered if we had a chance. With nothing in Hawaii holding me back, I quit my job, emptied my bank account, packed up my things and got on the plane. Eighteen years old and headed towards Hollywood . . . gosh, it sounded so good.

I arrived in Los Angeles with torn jeans, spiked hair and three suitcases. The pace of Hawaii had caused the world to slow down in such a way that Los Angeles seemed like a beehive gone mad. I felt like I had stepped into a marching band playing the fight song during a halftime performance. Tom, of course, was nowhere to be found. Change in hand and standing at the nearest payphone, I called and called and called the number he had given me. I certainly didn't have a cellphone and email hadn't been invented for public use yet, so my options were a payphone and a payphone. Back then men gave their word, not a cell phone number, and I held on to the promise that he would show up. Four hours later, my tears dried in layers, Tom sent a limousine which honked out my name as it pulled into LAX to find me. No stranger to big cities and with no change left to call Tom; I got into the car hoping the driver wasn't going to rape and kill me. What other choice did I have? I didn't know a single soul in Los Angeles and I sure as hell wasn't going to call my family and tell them that I needed their help.

It was a six-month relationship, and a seventeen-year age difference. What I slowly began to realize was that we only had one thing in common, and it wasn't God. Tom worked as an executive in one of the biggest software businesses in Los Angeles. I quickly realized that his life was not his own. She called him and then he called me, cancelling plan after best laid plan. I couldn't understand how a person could live at the whim of someone else all in the name of money. After a few months, I found myself doing the same — living with Tom for the creature comforts, and I slowly began to hate my life.

Tom was a kind man who used his Rolodex to get my foot in the door of any place that was hiring. Since Tom had connections on Rodeo Drive, he set up an interview at a high end department store, where we both thought I would be hired on the spot. I was dressed in black boots, white shorts, a green and white shirt and black suspenders. I looked like a circus freak show. The manager was dressed in an Armani suit with slicked-back hair, manicured nails and polished wing-tip shoes. Tom introduced us and left to go attend to his mega-million boss. Two minutes after Tom walked out the door I was thanked for coming and left at a coffee table where I melted into the floor. I became invisible for the next two hours as I waited for Tom to pick me up. It was one of the most humiliating days of my life, and it's what got me thinking about my future once again. Tom never came back to pick me up from that interview, telling me he would meet me at home after his work day was done. I got on the bus and headed back to the apartment to pack up my things.

I left LA with a note on Tom's dining room table, right next to the wine bottle he opened every night when he got home. With my three suitcases and dusty Bible, no hand lotion, an earring, makeup and spiked hair, I headed back to Montana once again, just a few months shy of my nineteenth birthday.

US NAVY

(Age 18)

From Montana to Bogota to Montana to Hawaii to Los Angeles and back to Montana once again, I felt the majestic grasp of the Rocky Mountains snatch me by the collar one more time. Upon arrival, my earring glistening in my left ear, bleach-blond hair screaming faggot and my makeup applied nicer than any of those girls at the Nordstrom counter, my father took one look at me and relegated me to live in the basement where I had a hideaway bed and a bathroom up two flights of stairs. I was quickly reminded that my father drove a truck to support us, goddamnit, and he didn't wear any makeup or earrings to get the job done. I tried to convince him that a left-eared earring meant I wasn't gay, but he knew my unspoken truth.

With my $85 dye job and a newly purchased cosmetic bag, I wandered around Missoula like a homeless person. I thought about going back to the Clark Fork Christian Center to see Pastor Valentine but after living an openly gay life in Hawaii and Los Angeles, I didn't have the energy to reconcile my past as I still wasn't sure what my past actions meant. Was being gay truly against the will of God? As a "saved Christian" I was taught that once saved I was always saved, so if I were suddenly killed I knew God wouldn't hold my confusion against me, but I wanted an answer to this puzzle. I knew I had same-sex attractions, but I hadn't reconciled how I could lead an openly gay life as a Christian, let alone in Montana. I was in no way ready to put the "faggot" sticker the kids had given me in the sixth grade back on my forehead. Church had been such a special place in my life and for the briefest of moments I had believed that my world, with God, was somehow complete. I could remember the contradiction of my private homosexual feelings and how they seemingly faded away into the ether, until I got honest with the Pastor. Now, standing on the street corner of Brooks and Higgins with my arms raised to shield the sun, God seemed as far away as the four years that had since passed. So, I passed by my old church day after day, hearing the words of Pastor Valentine: "God loves everyone, but homosexuality is a sin, and you have to change if you want God's grace." God's grace was framed in a choice; become straight or go to hell, a choice that felt as impossible as a grizzly bear turning into a butterfly. I didn't see how this choice was possible.

No savings, no pending college enrollment, no job and no car — I was fucked. Day after fucking day I lamented my life. My parents served meat for dinner, lectures for dessert and repeated advice for bed-time snacks. I wondered if my situation were proof that kids should stay at home and endure the difficulties of their teenage years so that when they were finally released they could explode onto the world scene in a shower of magnificence. My rocket had launched two years prior and now I found myself sitting on the launching pad with a malfunctioning engine. Stuck again in Montana, there wasn't an engineer in sight to help me light up and take off again.

Through the smoky haze of marijuana, cigarettes and my father's never-ending criticism, I somehow found a job as a sales clerk at one of those department stores where the floors creaked, the women at the perfume counter smelled like a whorehouse and the general manager did nothing but smile. I hadn't ever worked in sales before, but I loved the cardigan sweaters that they sold, so I sold myself to the manager and started working full time. Wrapped up in sweaters that made me look like a middle-aged man, I began peddling the wares of The Bon. It was close enough that I could walk or catch the bus, and it got me out of reach from my father's lecturing tongue. I was never going to be him, had no desire to be him, or live my life the same way as him. But, it was no use trying to tell him that because the answer was always the same. He drove a truck to support us, goddamnit, and that was all there was to it.

A few months into the job the cardigan sweaters tried to strangle me. I was bent over in the dressing room, picking up after some lazy kid who threw all of the clothes on the floor, and before I knew it I was face down struggling for breath. Sucking cotton at work and the cock of a guy getting his master's degree from the University of Montana at night, I knew I had to leave. Neither one fulfilled me, and selling clothes felt like selling out. South America constantly reminded me that I hadn't come this far with my life just to put a sales tag on my future and settle. It's the educated monied people who get to throw clothes on the dressing room floor and complain about the price clearly written on the tag.   Faye Dunaway had the right idea in beating those around her into complete submission, and when I found myself gripping the wire hangers a little too tightly one Sunday afternoon while explaining to the mothers of the self-entitled assholes that they did look a bit husky in the sweaters and jeans they had selected, I knew the end was near.

Missoula had one gay bar in town, Daddy's, a shameless name that embodied everything that I hated about the gay lifestyle. Daddy — really? I had nothing but contempt for my dad, and I had no desire to be with a daddy type, but there wasn't much choice if I wanted to connect with like-minded men, so I became a regular. Daddy's was my own personal sanctuary -- a place where I didn't have to pretend, where my family couldn't find me, and where I could let everything hang out and have fun. I was accepted, my youth was celebrated, and my current failures were drowned in a beer bottle. It was the only place I felt free — my past, current and future lives all coming together to dance with me instead of fighting about who said what and when. Daddy's was a place that validated my insecurities and boosted my self-esteem. God became a distant memory once the music started.

Sales clerk during the day and a barfly at night, the routine of my life slowly ground on my psyche like a rock stuck in a set of car brakes. With no motivation to mark clothes up or down, and even less to pick them up off the floor, I drove my car over to the military recruiter's office and decided that I would join the United States Marine Corps. It couldn't have been any worse than living with an alcoholic or an absent parent not to mention the retail job. Besides, I was one of the only kids I knew who could take a ninety minute aerobics class and then go out to the car and smoke a cigarette before heading back in to lift weights for thirty minutes. When I thought about it and then went home for a family dinner on Sunday night — a delicious gourmet meal of alcohol, tension and advice — I knew the Marine Corps was my answer.

Montana. Yes, a river runs through it along with loggers, logging trucks, pick-up trucks and people who visit from all over the world to hunt and fish. A cacophony of adventure, it was the perfect place to raise children as long as you were white, straight and believed solidly in capital punishment. Having left home at sixteen, I knew my destiny didn't begin or end in Missoula. My grandmothers were counting on me, both of them believing that the sun rose behind my back and set on my smiling face, and I couldn't let them down. I also couldn't tolerate the alcohol glass that my father couldn't seem to put down, my mother who couldn't seem to talk to me without putting me down or my sister who was perpetually down on her luck. No, Missoula wasn't going to be my future any longer, and so I was faced with no other option but to succeed, in the military.

Like dogs sniffing each other's butts for the answer, the main question after you join the military is, "Why did you join?" Lots of guys say that they want to serve their country, travel, get money for college and all of the other esoteric and noble things you might expect. Me? I wanted to get the fuck out of Montana. It really was as simple as that, as I hadn't ever thought about the military. I thought that only underachieving, crime ridden, troubled youth joined the military. I was, after all, a foreign exchange student who was fluent in Spanish and had been chosen by God the summer of my eighth-grade year. The military seemed like a choice that sold me short, and not a choice that I had prayed to God about, but it allowed me the opportunity to leave Montana. When I weighed one evil against the other, I knew my mind was already made up. I couldn't stay in Montana for it was eating at me like a terminal illness and I hadn't managed to reconcile my homosexual lifestyle with God, so what other choice did I have? The military recruiters were only too happy to talk to me and sign me up, which is what I did the very next day.

When I joined the military it was one of the few moments in my life when my father provided me with advice that I actually listened to. His advice caused a seismic shift in my charted course. Set to enlist in the Marine Corps, my father talked me into joining the Navy instead, and although I had never seen a ship or worn bell-bottom pants, I listened to his advice and then headed over to Butte, Montana to pick my job assignment. With my physical, test scores and paperwork complete, it all came down to job availability. I was told that I could become a linguist, but if I wanted to leave right away the Navy had a job opening to become a quartermaster on submarines. Huh? Submarines and a quarter what? Leaving immediately meant more to me than the job. So I took the assignment and went to get sworn in. I was desperate to leave Montana.

1987. That was the year I joined the US Navy, January to be exact. Without the internet or Google to find out about life on submarines or what the job of a quartermaster entailed, I had to rely on people's words to describe my future life for me, like a tribal story passed on from generation to generation. Before I left, I had to sign several documents stating I had never used drugs, I had never been convicted of a crime, and that I was not a homosexual. I had no idea the military was going to ask about my sexual orientation as I didn't think I could screw anyone in the workplace while in uniform. What did it matter what my sexual orientation was? The focus on sexual orientation was baffling to me, but that didn't stop them from asking.

I'm not much of a history buff, but it's important to understand just how paranoid the military was about the service of gay men and women in uniform. Prior to World War II, sexually active homosexuals could be prosecuted under the Articles of War. Although the first person to be discharged from military service happened in 1776, a formal policy was put in place around 1942. This policy was written by military psychiatrists who warned that "psychopathic personality disorders" make homosexual individuals unfit to fight. Psychopathic — now that's a strong word. I suppose if I got horny enough I could have probably been considered psychopathic, but the same could have been said about my heterosexual counterparts as well. What nineteen-year-old man doesn't lose his mind when it comes to hormonal desires? Unfortunately, in 1942 the only group targeted in the hormone race was homosexuals, and they stood to lose their careers and all of their benefits if found out.

In 1951, the military wrote a Uniform Code of Military Conduct, which served as a guideline of behavior for all persons in uniform. Article 125 forbids sodomy amongst all military personnel, and defines sodomy as any person who engages in unnatural carnal copulation with another person of the same or opposite sex or with an animal. Penetration, however slight, was sufficient to complete the offense. When you read that article, the military was very clear. Butt sex between any two people was forbidden, which included all of the heterosexual men in the world who wanted to get inside the tighter hole.

In 1953, President Dwight D. Eisenhower signed an Executive Order, 10450, citing espionage and counter espionage concerns, which prohibited federal employees from being members of a group or organization considered subversive. The order lists "sexual perversion" as a security risk constituting grounds for termination or denial of employment. Just in case you're still paying attention, homosexuality was considered sexual perversion.

One last important date worth mentioning is January 16, 1981. The Department of Defense issued Directive 1332.14, stating that "homosexuality is incompatible with military service" and that any service member who has "engaged in, has attempted to engage in, or has solicited another to engage in a homosexual act" will face mandatory discharge. America, the most advanced and industrialized nation in the world, remained one of the last countries to allow gays to serve openly within the armed forces. If you're counting, these are the countries that beat America to its own self-actualization: Australia, Austria, Bahamas, Belgium, Canada, Czech Republic, Denmark, Estonia, Finland, France, Ireland, Israel, Italy, Lithuania, Netherlands, New Zealand, Norway, Slovenia, South Africa, Spain, Sweden, Switzerland and the UK.

From the 1940s right through the year I enlisted in the Navy (1987) and beyond (2008), the Department of Defense had a proverbial hard on for homosexuals in every color, shape and size. In 1987, you didn't have to be caught with a dick in your mouth or penetrating another fellow to be given a pink slip from the military. All they had to do was suspect that you were homosexual, and with a little bit of creative paperwork, you could be kicked out of military service with an "other than honorable" discharge.

After I signed the paperwork to enlist in the Navy as a submariner, a volunteer assignment with a guaranteed slot to attend Quartermaster School (navigation), I had to sit with a man in plain clothes who went through the list of questions once again. I wanted to remind him that I had volunteered to serve our country, volunteered for the Submarine Force and volunteered to have my life taken in defense of our country. Volunteer — it remains the only way to get into the Submarine Force.

Every single time he asked me if I had ever engaged in or was currently engaging in homosexual activity, my heart raced and my pupils dilated. I was determined to leave the circumstances of my childhood behind. I wanted to live a life according to what I believed to be God's will, so when the question popped up, I stated what I wanted for my life — to be a heterosexual male.

BOOT CAMP

(Age 18 – 19; first 16 months in the Navy)

I was more frightened landing in Bogota, Colombia at age sixteen and not being able to speak the language than I was entering Boot Camp in Orlando, Florida. When the drill instructors rattled the trash cans on the floor at 5 a.m. on our first day of indoctrination, I knew there wouldn't be a maid delivering coffee and a bagel. Moron, dummy, dumbass — all the words I had heard at home and from the three female bullies at school -- my drill instructors clearly needed a lesson in intimidation. I ran, swam, did push-ups, sit-ups, marched and studied right along with everyone else. I was smart enough to know that I didn't want to be the center of attention, either at the top or the bottom. Versatile since my teenage years, my goal was to stay in the center of the pack and make it through those thirteen weeks unscathed.

I sported the bell-bottom pants and white round Dixie hat with aplomb. Dress blues, dress whites, working blues and working whites, the Navy had more uniforms than my mother's closet. Make no mistake; I did my best to honor Pastor Valentine and stayed firmly in the closet, focused on the tasks at hand. The only time I talked about my peter or anyone else's was when the guys started talking in the shower one day about their lack of erections. Apparently nobody had been able to get it up since we had arrived at Boot Camp, and several of them were convinced that the Navy put saltpeter in our food. The military swears that it's the rigors of Boot Camp that keep male urges in abeyance, and according to the shower talk, we were all obeying.

I attempted to obey the word of God and gain His blessings by attending church every Sunday. I knew that good works wouldn't get me into heaven, but I hoped beyond hope that my dedication to His word would prove worthy enough to allow me to graduate from Boot Camp and move forward with this career. I was too focused on the tasks at hand to attempt to reconcile my homosexual lifestyle with Him, so my prayers remained squarely in the camp of, "God help me make it through this." My life prior to the Navy had become like tires spinning out in a snow bank, and I needed this opportunity more than I had ever needed anything else. I don't remember anything about the military priest who fed us our Sunday bread, but I do remember that I was one amongst many who left with a wet face on Sundays. God and donuts from elderly women who felt sorry for us; Sunday was definitely my favorite day of the week.

Every single day found us with open showers, toilets without walls, and open berthing where everyone sleeps in one room in bunk beds. There's no privacy in Boot Camp. I suppose this is a good opportunity to get one thing straight. I don't need to look at your dick in the shower, I don't want to look at your dick in the shower, and nine times out of ten I don't want your dick in my mouth or my dick in yours. Gay men grow up around dicks, both in and out of the shower, and when I joined the military; I was focused on work, not your dick. I always marveled at the way Senator John McCain broadcast to the entire world that he was opposed to ending the ban on homosexuality in the military because it would mean cohabitation of dick lovers and pricks. News flash Senator — we've been around dicks as long as you have and we're just not as fascinated by them as you seem to be.

Big potty and the gas chamber were the two things I feared most as I made my way through those thirteen weeks. I suppose you should know my one big secret — I have a phobia about taking a shit in public. I mean, I hate to be so blunt about it, but there's no way around bathroom talk. Going big potty, #2, a floofer, a fluffer, the big one, the second act, a squatter, a sitter or a seater — I mean . . . seriously?

Boot Camp had toilets with no doors on them, so we were required to splay our ass cheeks on the toilet as the guys next to us did the same, and those shaving at the sinks in front of us could watch. This presented a real problem for me as I just can't seem to pull down my pants and do the duty unless I'm at home. On those rare occasions when I've been left with no other choice — either shit my pants or shit my pants, I wait until all of the passengers have boarded the train, the conductor has blown the whistle, and the train is moving, literally coming right out of the tunnel.

Sit? Not a chance. Instead, I hover like a watercraft skimming across the Florida everglades. My engine gasps a few times before all the air gets out of the pipes, and of course my knees swear up one side and down the other that they will be able to support this operation.

The bottom line? I didn't take a shit during the day, no matter how bad I had to go. I would wait until "lights out" was called and then I would quietly get out of bed and go into the bathroom to complete the task at hand. On the rare occasion I did have to sit side-by-side with someone else who clearly had a shitty phobia like me, there was no talking shit between us as we sat atop the sacred bowls. How women go to the bathroom together and chit-chat is beyond my comprehension.

Then there was the gas chamber. It was raining in Florida the day we marched up to the gas chamber, nothing more than a brick box with two doors. Once the drill instructor dropped the pellets onto the ground, we were instructed to "break the seal" on our masks, breathing in the gas, which is when the tearing eyes and coughing set in. This event lasted from three-to-five minutes, and after the seal on my mask was broken, I had to put the mask on the top of my head and stand there as snot and tears and phlegm flew out of my body faster than water squirting from a fire hydrant. Once outside, I continued to shake the snot from my face like a wet dog shaking water off its back. Big potty and the gas chamber. That pretty much defines my Boot Camp experience.

After thirteen weeks of reindeer games, I was ready to graduate. My shaved head had grown back like a chia pet, my waist had shrunk a couple of sizes, and my skin was as smooth as a baby's bottom. On the eve of graduation we were let out from behind the steel fence to greet our families who had flown in from all over the United States to watch us graduate, and my father and stepmother were no exception. I was filled with pride as I walked into my father's arms and grasped my stepmother's tear- stained hand. It was an experience they could relate to, a visible accomplishment for us to collectively celebrate as a family. It was the first time in my life my father saw me achieve something he could understand, and he celebrated my success with several glasses of wine at the Italian restaurant later that night. Determined not to let the past encroach on the present, I remained silent and enjoyed the moment. The completion of my exchange student year was more meaningful to me, but this experience never translated to my American family, so I allowed my military victory to be theirs. To celebrate, we all went to Disney World where I had a silver ring made with the words "NAVY" stamped out across the top to ride across my left hand.

Twenty-five years later I still have that ring — it sits on my nightstand, right next to my favorite watch.

As soon as I got out of Boot Camp as a freshly-minted seaman recruit (E-1), my military orders had me heading across the street to Quartermaster "A" school in Orlando and then on to Submarine School in Groton, Connecticut. The memories of push-ups, screaming Boot Camp instructors and covert trips to the bathroom at night became a distant memory. Quartermaster "A" school found me focused on graduating at the top of my class. We were told that whoever graduated with honors would have a "possible choice" of what ship they would be assigned to. Competitive since birth, I took their promise and ran with it for the next several months.

April 3, 1987. It was a day like every other. Hot, humid and early — that's how I defined my school life in Orlando. Up at 5 a.m., a few-mile jog outside, shower, tight formation march to the chow hall and then off to class to learn about celestial and every other type of navigation that was taught in Quartermaster "A" school. There was no such thing as GPS (Global Positioning System) in 1987, so we learned the basics of Loran-C, Omega and bottom contour navigation. At around 10 a.m., I was called to the back of the classroom to talk to an investigator from the Defense Investigative Service (DIS). I was told that he would be asking me a few basic questions to begin my security clearance process and determine my eligibility for a Top Secret/Sensitive Compartment Information (TS/SCI) clearance. Hey, that sounded simple enough, right? When I enlisted, I had answered all of the basic questions about drug use, delinquency and dick sucking; a few more questions seemed like a no-brainer. What could it hurt?   We were still talking 3,557 days later. It was a nine-year, eight-month and twenty-six-day conversation that changed the course of my life. I wouldn't ask you to believe me, except that I have every single piece of paper written about this investigation and a microfiche to back it up.

Not knowing anything about submarines, I had even less knowledge about what a security clearance was or why in the heck I needed one to navigate a submarine. Since this is a central theme and an important part of this story, this is where you really need to pay attention. A security clearance allows military men and women to gain access to information that, if revealed, could be helpful to our enemies, harm national security and at the most extreme, cause the United States to have a classified mission compromised (think the killing of Osama Bin Laden) or lose a war.

For military personnel who work within environments that give them access to sensitive information, a security clearance investigation is required. The investigation focuses on an individual's character and conduct, emphasizing such factors as honesty, trustworthiness, reliability, financial responsibility, criminal activity, emotional stability, and other similar areas. All investigations consist of checks of national records and credit reports; some investigations also include interviews with individuals who know the candidate and in my case, it included a personal interview as well. It's a long process, and the day I was pulled to the back of the classroom was the first step on the road to my clearance. There are three categories of clearances: Confidential, Secret and Top Secret. I needed a Top Secret clearance, but that's not all. When a person is going to work with information that is even more sensitive than Top Secret, they are required to obtain a caveat to their Top Secret clearance known as "Sensitive Compartmented Information" (SCI).

On that fateful day, April 3 1987, I was being interviewed for a Top Secret/Sensitive Compartment Information, a TS/SCI clearance. Remember that.

As I sat down to speak with the investigator, I heard Pastor Valentine's words and remembered the rule within the Uniform Code of Military Justice, both of which said homosexuality was admonished. Having rationalized that God had it wrong, I didn't see how the military could have it right. I was the same as every other man in uniform; fit, focused and dedicated to serving our country. I had volunteered my life to serve our country, and on top of that I had volunteered for the Submarine Service. You cannot get into the Submarine Force unless you volunteer yourself as the Navy will not assign you to this rigorous assignment without your consent. It was one of the few things the Navy couldn't make you do unless you wanted to do it, and I wanted to do it. What I didn't want was to be treated differently because of my sexual preference. I knew I was a homosexual, but the other men I served alongside all had private lives that didn't call their military performance into question, and I had decided that neither would mine. If we're being honest here, the Uniform Code of Military Justice says that heterosexual couples are not allowed to commit adultery or engage in any conduct that is unbecoming to their rank. From my perspective, the contradiction of any conduct unbecoming to their rank was as befuddling as the sins of the Bible. Broken rules and sins were all equal — one was not worse than the other. According to the UCMJ and the Bible, a sin was a sin, equal in the eyes of the law and God. I knew everyone had sinned, so how could my hidden sin be worse?

I stuck to my rationalization of sinful acts when the investigator began his initial interview which put the wheels in motion for me to obtain a TS/SCI. I was required to give the address of every place I'd lived or worked, the name of every person with whom I had lived or worked and every foreign national I had been in contact with. I had to provide dates, with no gaps in time, and list personal references so that my statements could be checked. It seemed like a hell of a lot of work for a routine investigation, but I complied, and then kept a copy of the list I gave him so I could reference it in the future. Before he ended the conversation, he asked me if there was anything he should know about me before he started the investigation. Anything at all that would force him to question my integrity or doubt the sincerity of what I had shared.

Like a car accident, I have watched this moment in slow motion a thousand times in my head. A kid from Montana who was more academic than athletic, who sang rather than shouted, a family more broken than a mosaic, who tried to leave home at sixteen only to return three years later and escape by joining the Navy, what was I supposed to say? How could I be honest with this man about everything I had been through? I was a thirty-year-old man in a nineteen-year-old body, and he was asking me if there was anything else he should know?

My mouth opened, closed, opened and then closed again. I could feel tears choking up in the back of my throat and welling up in my eyes. As my mouth opened again, the words tumbled out, making their way across the table and onto the investigator's notepad. I watched him write as I spoke about my quiet nature, the way I was bullied in grade school and teased in high school for the way I acted. I confessed my brokenness, stating that there were some kids who thought I may be homosexual. As soon as my words flew out of my mouth, I knew I had made a mistake. The following is the report, typed up by Mr. Outten, from the April 3, 1987 interview. If you've never read an official military report, get ready, because here is your first good look at how that interview went:

INTERVIEW WITH PETTY OFFICER TRIPP:

1. An interview of Seaman Recruit Tripp was conducted on 03 April 1987 as part of an Oriented Background Investigation. Mr. Tripp's security questionnaire was used as the basis for the questions and the interview required 35 minutes. Mr. Tripp is currently an E-1 assigned to Quartermaster School, Service School Command, Naval Training Center, in Orlando FL.

    Seaman Recruit Tripp advised that when he was young his parents underwent a terrible divorce pitting him against each parent. He said his mother poisoned him against his father by telling him bad things, and his father provided the same information against his mother. He said he felt alone and mixed up, to the point that he did not know where the reality was. Tripp said he decided to get away from both parents and contacted an organization known as World Experience. He said this organization exchanged students in foreign countries. He said he went to Bogota, Colombia, South America, as an exchange student from Aug 1984 – July 1985. While there, he said he resided with a family who is identified as the Rojas family. He said Mr. Rojas was a distributor of bathroom parts and provided him with room and board while residing in that country. He said that he had no encounters with any law enforcement agency or any difficulties while residing in that country. He said that he did not acquire any lasting relationship with any foreign nationals while residing in South America. Seaman Recruit Tripp said upon returning to Missoula, MT he resided with his mother and he obtained employment at MARS, Inc., as a telephone solicitor. He said he would like to point out that while at MARS, Inc., he had somewhat of a confrontation with a supervisor named Jessie, not further identified. He explained that he had encountered a problem and had requested the assistance of Jessie. When Jessie came over to assist him, Jessie placed his hand on his shoulder and helped him resolve the problem. Tripp said he felt uncomfortable with Jessie's hand on his shoulder and he asked Jessie to remove it. He said that Jessie subsequently reported this matter to a higher supervisor, who is Bobbie P., who asked him what the problem was. He told Bobbie what had happened and nothing more was said about it. He described Bobbie as being a lesbian and stated that he thought Jessie was a homosexual. Also, he is afraid of what both of them may say about him during a background investigation for a security clearance. Tripp also advised he has lived a quiet lifestyle, mostly by himself, not mingling with other people. He said because of his studious goals in life he devoted most of his time to his studies. He said that he seldom dated girls but he did date on occasion. Seaman Recruit Tripp said he had not participated in any of the sports programs while in high school. He said that he is not a joiner of any social organizations and a participant in those activities where a lot of people are present: however, he said he did join an actor's guild while in high school and that he participated in a few plays in the local area. Tripp stated that in June 1986, he decided to visit Honolulu, HI for a short vacation. He said while there, he fell in love with the islands and decided to remain there for the entire summer. He said he obtained employment. While in Hawaii he encountered no difficulties whatsoever. Tripp said he departed Hawaii in August 1986 and traveled to the Los Angeles, CA area. He said that while in California, he made up his mind to attempt to make it on his own without any assistance from his parents. He said he obtained employment in the Los Angeles, CA area as a phone solicitor. He said while residing in the LA area, he mostly kept to himself working during the day time and attending the gymnasium for a few hours at night, keeping in shape. He said that he departed LA in November 1986 and returned to Missoula, MT to reside with his father. Seaman Recruit Tripp voluntarily reported that he had a falling out with his mother that has resulted in a complete breakdown of their relationship. Tripp stated that he does not care to discuss anything further about his mother because he now considers that he does not have a mother. He said that he has acquired a good relationship with his stepmother, who understands him and who can relate to any problems he may have. Tripp declared that he is afraid of what other people may say about him to the Defense Investigative Service when conducting the background investigation. He said because of his quiet lifestyle and other factors, such as not dating girls as often as other males do, people may accuse him of being a homosexual. Tripp said that he has not done anything during his lifetime that he is personally ashamed of and certainly nothing that he could be blackmailed for by an enemy agent or a representative of some other country. Seaman Recruit Tripp denied that he has ever engaged in homosexual activity or that he has ever possessed any homosexual tendencies and vehemently denied being gay in any fashion.

By fashion I wondered if they meant couture or casual, because I did like to wear sweat pants when not in uniform and I liked them fitted, which technically makes them couture. From the sound of this report you would think that I was a military general, a four star to be exact, getting ready to lead 10,000 troops into battle. But no, I was just an E-1 — the lowest of enlisted military ranks — focused on the lofty goals of making sure the toilets and the floors were clean.

I never mentioned to Mr. Outten that I had switched host families in South America as I didn't want to try and explain how my host brother Carlos was really Marilyn Monroe posing as Hitler. As far as Mr. Outten and the investigation were concerned, I lived in South America, came home to Montana, attended my senior year of high school, got a job at MARS, and then moved to Hawaii and Los Angeles, all in a period of a few years. I didn't think they would send an investigator to South America to find out the full story, but I guessed wrong. The one thing I guessed right was that I needed to cover my ass about my job at MARS in Montana.

I got the job at MARS one month after I returned from South America and was hired as a telephone operator, a Spanish-speaking one who verified the green card status of immigrants. Jessie, a hunk of a man who has since passed away, was my supervisor. I first met Jessie at a gay soiree a few weeks after I came back to America and before I secured employment at MARS. The party was hosted by one of the university students I kept in touch with during the year I was an exchange student. When I went upstairs to toss my jacket in the "coat bedroom" imagine my surprise to find two men playing leap frog — Jessie and Dan. A seventeen-year-old kid, with my own car and my parents too busy fighting about their divorce to wonder where I was heading at 9 p.m., this night was an education on the wild side. I had never seen leap frog before and I wasn't sure if it was pain- or pleasure-filled, but it definitely got my attention. I filed it in my wank bank for future reference.

What I told Mr. Outten about Jessie putting his hand on me at work was absolutely true. What I failed to mention was that he also put his mouth, his tongue, and every other part of his body on me after the work lights were shut off. I fell in love with Jessie, my first real crush on a man. Work days with Jessie morphed into long rides up the mountain where we parked and enjoyed the moon. Yes, I was over the moon with him. Unfortunately, his leap frog partner, Dan, somehow found out and tried to get me fired, and he had the juice to get it done -- Dan just happened to be best friends with Bobbie, Jessie's supervisor. It was my first official foray into the wrath of another man and I quickly became persona non grata at work. Then one night, Dan found us in the loft at Jessie's house and tried to break in. I made a break for the door and hid in the field behind Jessie's house, sleeping on the ground until the sun came up. My parents never noticed that I didn't come home, which taught me just how much I could get away with during my last year of high school. I quit my job a few days later, and never spoke to Jessie again.

I suppose I could have told the investigator that story, but I didn't want to watch him shift uncomfortably in his seat, so instead I told him that Jessie made an advance on me, I reported it, and was then forced to quit. All of those things are true, but as you know, they don't tell the full story. Whatever relationship I had with Jessie was over, and since he wouldn't be joining me on the submarine, I didn't understand why the full truth, and nothing but the truth, was so critical. So, I told my story my own way, covering my ass in case Mr. Outten uncovered the real story.

Eighteen days later I was called back into the Defense Investigative Service office where Mr. Outten offered me a "chance to elaborate" on what my fears were regarding homosexuality. That fateful statement I made on April 3, 1987 had come back to haunt me. My fears? How about broken hearts, HIV, STD or better yet let's talk about how the military viewed homosexuals as unfit to serve because of a "mental illness." Let's start there. I didn't get enough mental abuse at home, and was really look-ing forward to the opportunity to explain myself, which is what I did for the next four hours. I was seated on a thick wooden chair in the center of the room. I had one interrogator (my word for investigator) behind me and one in front of me. They threw questions back and forth over my head, asking me to repeat the same thing I had just repeated and then I had to repeat it again. I wanted to ask them if they were hard of hearing, but it was clear that what they had were collective hard-ons to get me kicked out of the Navy for fraudulent enlistment. According to the Uniform Code of Military Justice, homosexuals were not allowed to serve, plain and simple.

Throughout the entire ordeal, I continually stated that I was not and am not a homosexual, but that wasn't good enough. They spent two hours "encouraging" me to write and sign a six-page statement outlining my move to South America as an exchange student, my dating in high school, our hosting of an exchange student named Johnny Alvarado, my employment at MARS, and to deny homosexual behavior in any and all situations. I wrote "I believe it to be absurd and discomforting that anyone would brand me or imply that I am a homosexual. I have done nothing to acquire this assumption. I defy anyone to produce substantial evidence that I am a homosexual." I repeated, both written and verbal, my desire to continue to serve in the Navy. I had to convince them that I was not a homosexual because they simply did not believe me.

After four grueling hours, I relented and wrote a statement filled with what I believed to be the truth as best as I could tell it without compromising my desire to serve our country. Homosexuality, while forbidden, was no greater transgression than that of other broken rules, and that is what I kept telling myself as I wrote the following statement:

21 April 1987 at 1300 hours is as follows:

I would like to add an additional residence while at Bogota, Colombia, S.A. When I departed Montana in August 1984 I lived at the home of Carlos H. He had one daughter and two sons. While living with them they resided at two different addresses. The first address was Calle XX and the second address was Carrera XX. I lived in their household from Aug to Nov 1984, at which time I began residing with the Rojas family. We lived at Calle XX. The reason I left the Carlos H. family is because one of the sons seemed to speak English most of the time and I did not have a complete family life as the family was gone quite often. It was my desire to be in a family that spoke Spanish all of the time, as I am fluent in the Spanish language. I wish to point out that the above is the ONLY reason I desired to change households while in S.A. I would like to state while living at any residence and at any household in S.A. there was NEVER any instance of impropriety wherein I had ANY confrontation with anyone or discussion whereby it was thought that I may be homosexual. Upon returning to MT I resided with my mother at her residence. To the best of my knowledge there was never any discussion with her about my being a homosexual. I have never possessed any homosexual tendencies nor have I participated or engaged in any homosexual activity. I did point out during my first interview with DIS that I thought perhaps there would be some persons interviewed who would think that I may be a homosexual. I would like to reiterate again this perception was due to my quiet lifestyle, my constant devotion to my studies and the absence of being popular with the girls. I would like to note that while in high school I did go out on several dates with girls and this can be documented by Pat P. and his family, friends and neighbors who now reside in Missoula, MT. Also I would like to point out the name of a person who can attest to the circumstances surrounding my changing residences while in S.A. This person is Ron Medor, who is the husband of my coordinator in Montana. Mr. Medor did in fact engage in a telephone conversation with my primary coordinator in South America. I cannot recall that coordinator's name, however, she was a female assigned to my school in South America. Regarding my association with Johnny Alvarado, who was a foreign exchange student from Costa Rica and who resided in my mother's home during the period of August 1985 – April 1986. From the very beginning I did not get to know Johnny Alvarado very well. We had different interests and personalities, he went his way and I went mine. I would like to point out the reason he moved from my home. During his stay in my mother's home, often times there were absences of anyone being at home. I was employed and spent most of my time away from home. My mother was also very busy and was away from the house quite often. Alvarado was left alone quite often and it was later discovered or established that Alvarado amused himself by throwing martial art stars at his bedroom walls. I believe it was April 1985 when my mother learned that he destroyed his bedroom walls which cost her about $600 to repair. My mother notified the exchange student authorities in Missoula, MT. After two weeks discussion between my mother and the authorities, it was concluded that Alvarado had to leave and was placed in another home in Missoula. I deny that I ever participated in any action whereby it could be interpreted by Alvarado that I ever suggested, demonstrated, participated, engaged in or led anyone to believe that I may have been a homosexual. Alvarado's departure from my mother's residence was entirely his doing and had NOTHING TO DO WITH ME. I would like to reiterate what transpired at my employment at MARS in Missoula, MT. As stated previously, I was concerned about what Jessie and Bobbie might say about me during the DIS Investigation. I thought that because I suspected them to be homosexuals themselves, they may stick together in testimony against me in saying that I was a homosexual. This of course is based upon a confrontation I had with Jessie when he placed his hand on my shoulder. At no time did I ever give anyone any reason to suspect me of being a homosexual during my employment at MARS. I would like to furnish names of two co-workers at MARS who would be in a position to attest to my moral character and reputation. They are identified as Lynne T. and Maria H. I believe it to be absurd and discomforting that anyone would brand me or imply that I am a homosexual. Again, I have done nothing to acquire this assumption. I defy anyone to produce any substantial evidence that I am a homosexual. I feel very comfortable in saying this because it would be impossible to do so, because I am as heterosexual as anyone. It is my desire to continue my career in the Navy and provide the Navy with any talents and cooperation that I possess. Mr. Outten assisted me in the preparation of this statement.

Good old Mr. Outten, what a champ. A four-hour interview and then a personal reach around to "help me" write a statement that could hang me out to dry should his investigative efforts find that I was indeed a young man struggling with homosexual desires. It was clear that he didn't believe me, and it was also very clear that since I wasn't sucking dick in front of Mr. Outten he had no business in my bedroom, and I was going to make sure he stayed out of it. My ability to navigate a nuclear powered submarine had nothing to do with whom I slept. Even I was smart enough to see through this argument, and so, argue I did, against any remote connection to homosexuality.

As I left the interview to head back to class, my palms were wringing wet. I remember saying a prayer to God, for prayers were all I had at that point. I had played tug of war between God and homosexuality for several years now; I had no desire to add military investigators to the mix. My lies were all I had — lies that felt authentic to my cause but inauthentic to the person I knew I was.

Secrets. My world was slowly starting to fill with a new set of secrets. I had kept the secrets of my alcoholic father, my sexual confusion, my love for God and the torture at school all wrapped up in brown paper bags, like the ones I took to school as a kid. I never liked to mix my vegetables and mashed potatoes together, everything had to stay completely separate and compartmentalized on my dinner plate, and my secret brown paper bags were no different. Every part of my life was separate to those who knew me and my technical acumen for compartmentalization was truly at the top of its game. One person knew one fact, another person knew another fact, but nobody in my life knew the entire story. When I looked in the mirror at age nineteen, what stared back at me was a broken young man.

With only a few weeks remaining before I left for Groton, Connecticut, I worked tirelessly to graduate at the top of my Quartermaster "A" school class. I couldn't afford failure. I couldn't afford the threat of being kicked out of the Navy for something I didn't fully understand about myself, and I sure as hell could not go back to Montana. My upset stomach was a constant reminder that danger was around every corner, so I kept a professional demeanor and a large personal distance between myself and everyone else. I graduated with honors and received the second highest grade in my class. The Navy packed me up and sent me off to Groton to attend Submarine School, but not before I was forced, again, to unequivocally deny any association with homosexuality.

SUBMARINES

(Age 19)

Long, black and with bodies hidden almost entirely underwater, my first impression of submarines was ominous. As I got out of the cab and walked up to the brand new set of brick buildings and freshly minted sidewalks, I felt intimidation rise up within me.

Groton is home to one of the largest submarine bases and is affectionately known as "rotten Groton," a nickname that has more meanings than Webster's dictionary. I had trumpeted my new adventure to everyone back home, making sure I captured the full mystery of what a submarine represents, like Batman describing The Joker. Like it or not, I was going onboard a submarine for the next three and a half years of my life. I had gone down plenty, but never underwater, so this was definitely going to be a new experience and one I couldn't get out of unless I flunked out of Submarine School. The thought of going back to Montana with no chance at a future was enough to choke the fear from my throat back down into my stomach and afforded me the opportunity to tap into a laser-like focus I didn't know I had.

Basic Enlisted Submarine School (BESS) is a test of academic endurance combined with firefighting and a water endurance "trainer." Up at 5:15 a.m., class began at 7:00, an hour for lunch and school ended at 4:00. We were given a two-hour break to eat dinner and rest, and then get back to the classroom at 6:00 for a three-hour study session, which put us in bed at 10:00 p.m. The instructors warned us that our days would be long and the information would challenge each and every one of us, and they made good on their promise. We did nothing but eat, breath, drink and piss submarine data.

When a young enlisted man walks on board his first submarine, he is known as a NUB (non-useful body). It typically takes each person around nine months to "qualify" on all of the sub's systems. The qualification process is the only way that a man becomes useful to the crew, and the NUB is not allowed to watch any movies or do anything on his free time other than study. Finishing the qualification process identifies a man as someone whom the other members of the crew can depend on to save their lives. In order to finish, you have to acquire signatures from each crew member who is already "qualified" on the system, and when they sign your qualification card it means that this crew member believes you have the required knowledge to go on to the next system. Once all of the signatures are obtained, the sailor is then required to pass a written and verbal exam, which can last up to four hours. If he passes, he is deemed "qualified" and is given his dolphins — a momentous day in the life of any submariner! I still remember the day I received my dolphins as clear as the night my father left for good, and my mom changed the locks on the house within the hour.

Submarine School is the beginning of the long and dusty road to becoming "qualified." Students must be able to grasp the concept of every system onboard submarines, and then be able to explain and draw them in order to pass. The failure rate is very high, and classes typically graduate with a much smaller class size than they started with. Submarine School runs by the second, not by the minute, and every single second counts. The color grey does not exist. Everything is either black or white — there is no room for middle ground or a loose interpretation of facts on a submarine. Things are either right or they are wrong, and there is only one correct way to accomplish tasks. For those who cannot grasp the educational material, realize they are claustrophobic or do not understand that the rules cannot be broken, they are asked to leave Submarine School without as much as a dolphin kiss goodbye.

I submerged myself into my school work, determined not to fail. Unfortunately, I had a nagging hangnail left over from Quartermaster "A" school, namely the Defense Investigative Service. As I was busy studying, Mr. Outten was busy writing. On May 4, 1987, just thirteen days after I made my written statement, Mr. Outten wrote up a summary of his findings. An important fact that shouldn't be overlooked is that the only time I gained insight into what the investigators were finding out about me, thinking or strategizing is when they pulled me in to interview me. All of their "filed" reports weren't revealed to me until several years later. They are included here in chronological order so you can grasp the severity of the situation, which I knew was grave, but didn't have the benefit of these reports, like you. For a kid trying to succeed in submarines by studying and working his ass off, these interviews felt like traveling in a car and then hitting a wall at 80 mph. I hoped with all the hope I had that this would go away, but it never did, and every single time I was called in to have a chat my world spun upside down as I listened to the facts and questions the investigators teased me with. A quick thinker, I was forced to answer their questions on the spot, in the moment, without wavering, without any doubt, and without knowing what they knew or didn't know. To appear weak was to give credence to what it is they found, and I knew if I did that, it would be the end of my career.

You may be wondering why in the hell I didn't tell the investigators and the US Navy the truth and just allow myself to be kicked out -- right? I suppose today this sounds like a plausible option, but in 1987, it was a reality that I could not accept. To admit being homosexual would have been admitting failure, and like Rosa Parks, I wasn't going to sit at the back of the bus because some rule stated that this is what was required. I knew I had to stay in the Navy if I were going to succeed; my parents made that abundantly clear when they refused to pay for my college or assist me in becoming a man. I had no close friends to rely on, South America taught me that hard work does equal success, and I had no desire to become a bartender at a local gay bar in a tropical town. The rule of not allowing gay people to serve did not make sense to me. Again, and I will probably say this a hundred times, but if I wasn't having intercourse with another man while at work, in uniform, why did it matter what my sexual preference was? There were plenty of men and women who were violating the Uniform Code of Military Justice in the bedroom (think adultery), and my situation didn't seem any more egregious than theirs. I knew I could do the job and I couldn't go back to Montana. I was going to stay in the Navy and that's the only option I allowed myself to consider.

It was difficult for me to understand how a lie about my sexuality could influence my life's destiny. I was so desperate to get out of Montana and make something of myself, especially after my successful year in Bogota that I was willing to be authentic to the truth I understood, while being inauthentic to the person that I really was. I didn't have the insight to piece this concept together until much later, for at age nineteen I stood on principle — squarely on top of the box of "fuck you, you can't do that to me." I considered the word of God to be a guide for my life, but when it came to homosexuality, I didn't believe anyone had the right to tell me if I was right or wrong. I believed the decision of righteousness regarding homosexuality resided squarely on my shoulders. The bullying I endured had provided me a mouthpiece of courage that I didn't know I had.

So, as I was busy studying away, Mr. Outten was busy writing his findings which were accomplished through personnel interviews, police reports and of course, my grade point average at Submarine School — a healthy 93.9, no easy task. As suspected, Mr. Outten didn't find me copulating in my grade school parking lot or handing out blow jobs to the basketball team. But he did uncover a man named David who had told the investigator that I went to him and confessed my homosexuality.

David hosted all of the exchange students at his house prior to our departure to our respective countries. I was so focused on leaving for Bogota, that my "exchange student familiarization" weekend was nothing but a blur. I knew it happened, but I couldn't tell you what happened. Our group spent the weekend talking about our fears, our hopes and our desires for the year that awaited us. Fast forward three years and that same gracious host, who had been interviewed as part of the TS/SCI investigative process, had told the investigators that I had confessed my homosexuality to him. WHAT? I didn't even remember what this man looked like let alone remember that we had shared an intimate conversation about my sexuality. I was many things at age sixteen, but I was not the kind of young man who would openly discuss a sexual issue at an exchange student retreat.

I wasn't privileged to any of this information until I was confronted by the investigators. Again, you have the privilege of seeing all of these documents at once, and David's written statement caused a full scale ruckus within the investigative unit adjudicating my case. Unbeknownst to me, the investigators were back to sniffing the trail of my past, convinced that they had indeed found the gay scent that I had somehow left behind. The following is David's statement:

Statement from David:

Special Agent Jenkins has assisted me in the preparation of this statement at my request. My association with Paul Tripp was as an acquaintance with only several contacts. I am also gay. I first became acquainted with Tripp at a party for World Experience host-ed by Donna at my present address (in Spokane, WA) during the summer of 1984. My next contact with Tripp occurred about fall 1985 upon Tripp's return from Colombia. I observed Tripp at a Mis-soula, MT gay bar "Daddy's," dancing with three to four other gay men in the course of an evening. The "Daddy's" bar is primarily a gay bar, however, there were also mixed crowds comprised of col-lege students. I initially viewed Tripp as somewhat attractive, how-ever, I perceived him as also promiscuous in his sexual contact with other gays and it was for this reason that I had nothing to do with him, as I was concerned about the possibility of acquiring AIDS. I have no affiliation with World Experience and only know Don-na from prior odd jobs; i.e., cutting lawns. There is no doubt in my mind that Tripp is gay. The only other people acquainted with Tripp being gay are Mike J., (and the rest is blurred and unreadable).

In 1987, people were allowed to hypothesize about things like sexu-al orientation, ruining a person's career. David's statement was used as a launching pad for what happened next.

The date was May 26, 1987. I was pulled out of Submarine School by the Defense Investigative Service so I could be interviewed by Mr. Carter. Apparently, Mr. Outten was only assigned to cases in Orlando, so I was lucky enough to get to tell my entire story all over again, to a new investiga-tor in Groton –– Mr. Carter. He wanted to know more about Hawaii, and having been through this hula dance before, I continued to stick to my no-dick-sucking defense. I suppose I failed to mention that I worked in a gay bar in Hawaii washing dishes and tables, didn't fuck any of the customers, tried acid, laid out in the sun slathered with baby oil and walked the beach at night wondering when my true love would find his way to me. Those details didn't seem relevant on that blustery Connecticut day, so I just stuck to the facts as I remembered telling them to Mr. Outten in Orlando.

My new investigator, Mr. Carter, was what I call a grill master. As he fired questions, I imagined him in a chef's apron, skewers in hand, prod-ding and poking the innocent steaks on the grill just to watch their blood run. He was the kind of guy who would let the steaks sit on the grill, until he deemed they were ready, regardless whether the juices ran clear or not. He was a pit bull of a man, and he wasn't going to let me out of the room until I answered the questions to his complete satisfaction. With my Submarine School coursework silently slipping beneath the surface of forgotten knowledge, I tried to hurry him along, but he just kept on humming and prodding and poking. I started from the beginning and just kept on tap dancing my way across his office, recounting every blessed detail, to include David's accusations, until he felt satisfied. Of course I didn't remember dancing at the gay bar "Daddy's" after I returned from South America. I was drunk — who can remember anything when you're drunk and having a good time?

Four hours later, I was released from the tongs of Mr. Carter. I remember heading back to my barracks room telling my instructors that I didn't feel well. The web of half-truths I had just unpacked in Mr. Carter's office had worn me down to a nub, literally. I sat on the edge of my bed and sobbed. There was no way I could face getting kicked out of the military; either to my family or myself. I was never going back to Montana; wild horses couldn't drag me back there, and yet, my future seemed so fragile. I knew the investigators didn't believe me which made me stick to my story with conviction stronger than super glue. I had no idea what they knew or didn't know, but I knew that they must have known something, or they wouldn't have kept coming back to question me. I believed I had covered all angles of my story, and my child of an alcoholic was working overtime to hide the truth and fabricate the best plausible story I could.

With Mr. Carter's investigation over, and unsure when I would be called back in for more questioning, I did my best to pass my final academic examinations and with one week left of Submarine School we were collectively faced with the firefighting and water endurance "trainer." The chatter from the upper-class is that both were scary, and if you failed either one of them you would be dismissed from Submarine School and be forced to go to a surface ship instead. I mustered up all of the strength I had inside of me, focused on Mr. Outten's and Carter's investigations and poured my anger into success.

No amount of anger could have doused the waves of water in the "trainer." This contraption is a giant cylindrical vault which required us to climb down a ladder into a makeshift "belly" of a submarine and wait as more than 20,000 gallons of water sprayed out of twelve leaks. There are cameras above and a bevy of instructors sitting behind glass windows with windshields, watching it all happen. The water starts as a dribble and turns into a gushing waterfall in a matter of several minutes. The objective is to stop the leaks, which is impossible, while maintaining a calm demeanor. It's more of a test of mental endurance than it is of actual skill. Let's be honest, if a submarine springs a leak while it is submerged in the ocean, it's going to be one hell of a mess. With my classmates standing on my shoulders and me on theirs, we did our collective best to stop the water and keep our wits about us. Needless to say, nobody from our group failed.

From water to fire, the instructors were standing by as we grasped our hoses and moved forward to spray at the flames. I daydreamed about the fire I had started with my admission that others might think I was gay in high school, wanting those words to be washed away, along with this troubled investigation. Unfortunately, the fire was now raging beyond my control, and the only thing within my realm of control was the fire right in front of me as we worked to put it out. Hot as blazes, we worked in teams, and within the allotted timeframe we achieved success. We only had one young man dropped from our group that day, a kid who decided he couldn't live under the ocean. I wasn't sure I could either, but the prospect of returning home was greater than my fear of a submarine.

As I rounded the final bend on Submarine School and prepared to move to Norfolk, Virginia to join the submarine crew of the USS CIN-CINNATI (SSN-693), another Defense Investigator, Mr. Anderson, was hard at work on my TS/SCI clearance. So now there were three, Mr. Outten, Mr. Carter and Mr. Anderson. Unbeknownst to me, on June 5, 1987, Mr. Anderson filed a report with the Defense Investigative Service which was made available to me several years later. According to this report, Mr. Anderson contacted a Mr. Medor who worked with the World Experience organization in Missoula. After I returned from South America, Mr. Medor contacted the regional World Experience office in Salt Lake City and spoke to a Donna. Mr. Medor stated that his initial understanding of my need to change host homes in Bogota, Colombia was due to a language issue with one of the sons at the first home. Donna informed Mr. Medor that I changed homes due to some sort of homosexual related issue.

It's true that I had confronted my host brother in South America about his sexual orientation as a way of blackmailing him into treating me as a member of the family, and it backfired. I was forced to switch families, and well, you know the rest of the story. I didn't reveal this fact in any of the investigations as it didn't seem relevant. With my sexual orientation being dragged through the mud for questioning, I wasn't going to bring up my host brother's conflict and I wasn't going to endure any questioning about possible sexual encounters with him. It was clear to me that the exchange student coordinator in Bogota had called Salt Lake and talked with Donna, who had now relayed her understanding of the story to Mr. Medor who had passed it on to the Defense Investigative Service. First David, then Mr. Medor and now Donna — the messy experience of growing up as an exchange student had now wormed its way into my TS/SCI clearance investigation even though none of what happened in South America had anything to do with my current military performance or occupation.

I remember a Navy Captain telling me that words have meaning, and it is clear that in the case for my TS/SCI clearance the words of David, Mr. Medor and Donna caused a firestorm in my life, which you have yet to discover. Was this injustice or justice? I'll let you decide.

Back to Submarine School, I had passed the academic rigors but not the rigors the investigators still wanted to put me through, as they would not go away. Fourteen days after speaking with Mr. Carter, aka Grill Master, yet another report was filed from yet another investigator — all on my behalf. This report was filed on June 10, 1987 by a Mr. Childs. Mr. Childs detailed his contact with Donna, the administrative secretary for World Experience. She stated that while I was at orientation and sharing my childhood experiences I stated that I was a very sensitive person and some people teased me about acting like a homosexual. Donna stated that I appeared to be a "sensitive person" but she did not observe or hear any admittance by me concerning homosexuality. This investigator also went back and spoke with David, who stated that while he was not sufficiently acquainted with me, he would appear at a hearing if necessary.

If you've lost count of how many investigators were working to uncover my sexual preference, the count is now up to five. Five federal employees conducting interviews, filing reports, calling people, obtaining statements and gathering evidence to be used in a possible hearing against me. Five investigators talking to an administrative secretary who said that I was a sensitive person and an old queen who was bitter about not being able to get into my pants. The Defense Investigative Service was really on top of their game at this point. Taking furious notes about every supposed statement I made and every man who ever wanted to sleep with me, these findings were enough to classify me as an enemy of the state. And this was only the beginning.

USS CINCINNATI SSN-693
(Age 19-20)

July 1987 was like every other month in Norfolk, Virginia –– hot as hell and as muggy as one of those big fat coffee mugs you find at Starbucks. Norfolk was the last place any sailor wanted to get stationed, and I had the great fortune of being assigned to the world's largest US Navy Base on my very first assignment.

To keep things simple, there are two kinds of submarines: Fast Attack (Los Angeles Class) and Boomers (Ballistic Missile). A Fast Attack submarine has one crew and can perform multiple missions from open-ocean Anti-Submarine Warfare to surveillance and intelligence gathering in the preparation/prevention of regional crises. Fast Attack submarines can transit at high speeds, undetected, independent of sea state, and arrive on station ready for action. Ballistic Missile submarines, or Boomers, have two crews (blue and gold), are designed for stealth and avoid detection at all costs. Boomers have a mission of nuclear deterrence.

If you were to put these two submarines side by side it is akin to comparing lingerie to big girl panties. Each serves a purpose, but one is a hell of a lot sexier than the other. I, Seaman Recruit Tripp, was ordered to report onboard a fast attack submarine (think lingerie) in July of 1987, at the tender age of nineteen.

With every life's possession packed into my sea bag, I made my way down the long concrete plank where several submarines were moored. My heart was racing, I was sweating up a storm in the hellish heat of Norfolk as my eyes scanned back and forth, looking for the USS CINCINNATI SSN-693. I had recently purchased a pair of boondockers (a clunky pair of black boots), which were stiff around my ankles. It's no surprise that I tripped and fell on my way down the plank, tearing a gaping hole in the knee of my dress white uniform. That's how my first official day on the USS CINCINNATI SSN-693 started.

I eventually found my way to the Cinci-fish and was greeted by the Chief of the Boat (COB), who was the highest ranking enlisted man on board the submarine. In layman's terms, the COB manages all of the enlisted men onboard, the Executive Officer (XO -- second in command) manages all of the officers onboard and the Captain (CO) manages every single person on the submarine, to include the COB and XO. The chain of command on a submarine is set in concrete; everyone has a mission, an assignment and a purpose. There's not a man onboard who doesn't serve a function, and as the newest and greenest guy on the sub, my job was to learn about navigation, scrub floors, clean toilets, get coffee and . . . study.

Submarines are akin to a prison that moves with grace, complete with "Yes Sir," "No Sir," "Aye Aye Sir" and "Right Away Sir." I discovered the zero tolerance for bullshit policy when I was slapped across the face for talking back. We were underwater, I was talking back, and the COB was having none of it. Before I could say Jiminy Cricket, his hand cracked across my face, tears sprung to my eyes and he didn't say another word to me. Instead, he turned his head away from me and stared straight ahead as if nothing had happened. It happened once more a few months later, and after that, it never happened again. Older men train the younger men and they were going to do whatever it took to make sure their lives were safe and the mission was accomplished. It wasn't personal, but I learned that I had better be a straight-up professional, or the consequences were going to be stiff, just like COB's hand. I can recall those moments as vividly as the day my dad caught me masturbating -- stark reminders that our private thoughts can cause us to demonstrate behavior in public that we don't always appreciate. In any event, living under the ocean is serious business and even though choking the chicken is standard practice, it isn't discussed. The men on board submarines focus mainly on one topic -- work.

Unlike a surface ship which has the ability to house its sailors, submarines are not equipped to allow anyone to live on them full time when they are in homeport, which in my case was Norfolk. When we were in homeport, the junior crew lived in a dorm type building, which we called barracks. I was put in a room with three other men, and we shared bunk beds along with a common bathroom for every person living on our floor. Each respective submarine is given a floor in the barracks, so the crew can live together. I lived in the barracks all three years and three months I was stationed on the USS CINCINNATI SSN-693. When we deployed for longer than a few weeks, we were required to move all of our things out of the barracks and put them in a storage facility, so another submarine crew could take over our floor. Life on a submarine is about rotation; you are either in homeport, you are out at sea training for a deployment or you are deployed on an extended deployment. Your entire life is beholden to the mission of the submarine. Unlike every other job in America, you belong, literally, to the submarine.

To give you a sense of the commitment it takes to make a submarine function, the crew works in eighteen hour shifts when under the water. Crew members work six hours on their station, which for me meant navigating the submarine for six hours, and then the remaining twelve hours are set aside to work, study and sleep. A typical submariner sleeps between four and six hours during their twelve hours off, and it's very common for the young men who have to keep the engineering department running like a clock to sleep every other eighteen-hour shift. If you're not qualified, sleep is viewed as a luxury, not as a necessity. Your qualification status is posted in the middle of the submarine for everyone to see and keep tabs on your progress. Teamwork is paramount, so the peer pressure is at a constant boil.

When in port, crew members are required to spend the night on the submarine every third day, which is called a duty day. Duty days require crew members to stand watch in four-hour shifts, which means that sometimes you are up all night and then required to work the next day. To give you an example of the rigors of this, if you have duty on Monday you will most likely be up most of the night, work all day Tuesday, go home and then work all day Wednesday and then come back on Thursday to spend the night on the submarine and do it all over again. Three days pass so quickly, I wonder why three is still my favorite number.

All of this talk of work at sea and on land begs the question as to which life is better for a submariner — the life underwater working eighteen-hour shifts or the life in port in where you are required to work for twenty-four hours every third day. Both are as uncomfortable as setting up a tent in a lightning storm; relentless, unforgiving and seriously taxing on the psyche. There were times I loved the peacefulness of being under the water, and yet the nights I was able to go out and party in any port I was in was a little slice of heaven.

If I wasn't working, I was alone searching for life's meaning on the dance floor. I became one of those men who disappeared into the night, lost in my own private paradise of music, men and mixed drinks. I used to walk into clubs, get a drink, quite possibly a smoke and then hit the dance floor for several hours, only stopping to go out to the car to change my sweat-soaked shirt. Yeah, I wanted sex, but I needed to mentally escape more than I needed to get my dick sucked. Bars, specifically gay bars, were where my self-esteem moved back into the "I'm hot" category of how I understood myself. Like Cinderella waiting for the clock to strike midnight before I had to put my uniform back on, I danced and I danced and I danced for as long as the DJ would spin the music. Short on conversation, I probably sacrificed a lot of mind-blowing sex for music, but I knew that if I didn't allow my steam valve of frustration to blow, I might just blow a gasket under the ocean, and that's a risk I couldn't take. Music became my savior on land, and God became my savior under seas.

I remember the first time I submerged beneath the murky deep. I was standing in the control room, the operational belly of the submarine, and I was watching the navigation team at work. One guy was on the periscope identifying a three-point fix on fixed landmarks, while the primary plotter laid down the bearings that were called out. It was a flurry of activity that happened every three minutes for hours on end. As long as the submarine was on the surface, the navigation team was in place. Submerged, it was up to one man to chart the course using all of the tools at his disposal. For now, it was my job to watch and learn.

The diving alarm trilled out that gorgeous tone, a cross between the honk of an old car horn and the muffled cry of a seagull, and before I knew it I could feel the submarine moving beneath the waves. I was as nervous and as quiet as a church mouse. My palms were moist, my brow was sweating and I could feel perspiration running down the back of my uniform. The leader of the navigation division, Quartermaster First Class Michael Benton, looked over at me and said "take a deep breath Tripp, it's as easy as sitting on an airplane." I won't ever forget those words.

Flying in an airplane takes a lot more faith than living on a submarine. Filled with people who don't read the safety instructions, have no idea how to operate the inflatable slide nor would they know how to get the emergency door open in a pinch, airplanes are death traps compared to living underwater. Submarines are as orchestrated and precise as a ballet troupe.

Everyone on a submarine has an exact role, they know when to execute it, they are trained as a team and if there's a catastrophe, everyone knows what to do. The beds on submarines are two feet wide, two feet high and six feet long, much bigger than any middle seat on an aircraft. Submarines make fresh bread daily, have an unlimited supply of the newest movies and afford you the opportunity to learn -- now tell me where you can find that on a 747! If you can wrap your head around the fact that you're surrounded by nothing but water, the rest of life on a submarine is manageable.

Although there are 130+ men onboard, not everyone is out of bed at the same time so the living conditions aren't that cramped. When everyone is up at the same time, I have to admit that a person's personal space is severely restricted. Intimate without intimacy, standing nose to nose with another man is not uncommon. Much like that infamous middle seat, a few hours into the adventure and you begin to feel like you have more room than you had before, and by the time it's time for everyone to go back to bed, you feel quite lonely when everyone leaves. Working in shifts, you might not see another person for several days. That's the dance of submarines.

As a Quartermaster, I was assigned with providing the Captain the submarine's exact location at all times. In 1987, we used periscopes, satellite fixes, celestial navigation and amplitude modulated signals (LORAN-C and Omega) on the surface, and a fathometer (bottom contour navigation) or time/speed/distance equations when it was submerged. Like everything else, times have changed and today the quartermasters of the submarine fleet use GPS to find their way. But back in the day, we were like every other person on earth who had to climb a hill both ways to and from school.

As I was learning my way onboard the USS CINCINNATI (SSN-693), the Defense Investigative Team was hard at work planning its next interview with me. From July 1987 until February 1988, I heard nothing but silence from the investigative team as it fanned out across my past, digging up as much information as it could. I was busy digging into the study guides trying to become "qualified" in submarines so I could receive my dolphins and be recognized as an official member of the crew. While I had graduated from coffee duty, I was still hard at work learning the navigational ropes, scrubbing floors and yes, cleaning toilets. Those illustrious jobs were going to stay with me for as long as it took for me to get qualified, and I was working at a feverish pace.

February 29, 1988. I was now twenty years old and just two months shy of my twenty-first birthday. I had been in the Navy for two years, onboard the USS CINCINNATI SSN-693 for six months, and we were getting ready to head out to sea for six months. It was a typical work day for me. We gathered in the control room at 6 a.m. and began work preparing navigational charts, ordering equipment and going about our daily tasks. At 9 a.m. the ship received a phone call and the Navigator walked up and told me that I needed to report to the Naval Intelligence Command at 10 a.m. He asked me what this was about and I told him that I thought it was a meeting to finalize my Top Secret clearance and with that, he let me go.

The Naval Intelligence Command is different from the Defense Investigative Service and it's a bit like comparing the FBI to a local police department. I had no idea of the difference until I walked up the front sidewalk of the Naval Intelligence Command and smelled the intensity. A stoic, non-smiling, hair-in-a-bun, wire-rimmed-glasses secretary greeted me and told me to sit down. No smile, no Diet Coke, no please or thank you. Clients who walked through this door were clearly guilty until proven innocent. Not knowing what had been uncovered, I knew my investigation had reached a new level of suspicion. Once again, I recalled the facts as I had told them to the Defense Investigative Service. Boot Camp, Quartermaster "A" School, Submarine School and now studying for my qualifications onboard the USS CINCINNATI SSN-693, my mind was whirring from information overload. I had moved to three different states, completed three assignments and was currently assigned to an attack vessel all in a matter of twenty-four months. The details of my past were as fuzzy as my father's memory after a few drinks.

On my third drink of water, my head swirling, I heard my name called like an accusation of theft. The gentlemen who escorted me into a windowless room with double mirrors and a microphone on the table gave me his name and told me that he was there to ask me a few questions. Questions . . . that's all my life was up until that point. Why was my father an alcoholic? Why did my parents pit me against each other in the divorce? Why did I like men? Did God really believe that homosexuality is a sin? Was Pastor Valentine right about my eternal damnation? Would I ever get qualified in submarines? Will I get kicked out of the Navy? My hands slid across the table leaving a film of sweat.

Mr. John P. Edwards was the acting director of the Naval Intelligence Command that day, a fact I discovered when I read the transcript of what happened. The names of the two agents who interviewed me are not legible on the transcription, and you can't possibly expect me to remember their names as I was having enough trouble remembering my own. What I do know is that my interview lasted close to six hours. Six hours of questions, answers, more questions, more answers, questions about my answers, answers to their questions and then the same questions all over again.

I didn't know what they knew and I was hoping that they didn't know what I knew, but who knew? Only those two gentlemen knew for sure, and they were playing their cards so close to their chests that not even the light from the fluorescent bulbs hanging above were able to sneak a peek. After several hours of banter they asked me to take a polygraph test. I wasn't giving them what they thought they knew, and since I had no idea what they knew, I knew I just had to keep repeating the same things over and over again. This, however, wasn't good enough. Again, I was asked to take a polygraph test to confirm my sexual preference. I remember asking them if it wouldn't be easier to bring in a Playboy and a Playgirl to judge my erection as a basis for arousal, but they denied my request. I thought it was actually quite clever since I could get aroused by both, one so innocently posed and the other so masculine and strong. With my hormones still at full tilt, visual stimulation by either sex ignited my imagination. I knew I could perform the task at hand if they would have only given me a shot instead of shooting me down. I promised I wouldn't shoot — but they clearly had a different target in mind.

A polygraph test translated into Basic English means a lie detector test. Did I say yes the first time they asked? No. I declined the test stating that I had to talk to some people and investigate the validity of the polygraph.

Scared? I was scared shitless, literally. My phobia of having to take a big potty right there was completely removed as I was too scared to move from my chair. I had one agent behind me and one in front of me. I'm not sure when I thanked my father for coming home drunk every single night, but the gift of his alcoholism taught me that I should stick to my story no matter how angry he got. To give in meant the gift of his temper, and so I always said the same thing over and over, no matter how angry he became. Unfortunately these agents weren't drinking, drunk, or believing my story. I stuck to it, hour after hour after hour after hour after hour after hour. It wasn't until the very end that I said yes to the polygraph test, at which point they let me get up and leave, assuring me that they would schedule my polygraph test within the next few days.

A few days, a few weeks, a few months — this investigation had been ongoing for almost two years. The incongruence of my top-notch work performance butted up against an unrelenting investigation caused the anger to well up in me, driving me to work harder, longer and with more success. I realized that I wasn't going to convince them of my truth or any truth other than the one they wanted to believe. My last hope was to work harder and smarter than everyone around me, so when the axe fell from above, and I knew it was going to fall, I would be saved at the last minute by a senior military person who believed in my abilities more than he/she cared about prosecuting someone for their "suspected" sexual orientation. That was the strategy I formulated for myself as I drove back to my submarine to get ready for a six-month deployment. Now, all I had to do was wait for the axe, which was in my estimation at least six months away. It would be difficult for them to give me a polygraph test underwater and the submarine was weeks away from deploying. I hoped against hope that we would pull away from the pier and dive underwater before they could pull me back in for a polygraph test.

DEPLOYMENT AND BACK AGAIN
(Age 19-20)

The submarine smuggled me out of America before the Naval Investigative Service could grab me for a polygraph examination. Gibraltar; Sardegna, Italy; Naples, Italy; Haifa, Israel; Toulon, France and seventy-two days straight of living underwater, that was my life from February 1988 to August 1988, highlighted by the successful completion of my qualifications, and some unexpected intimacy.

We had been working together for several months, ever since the submarine pulled away from the coast of the United States. I'm going to be honest and tell you that I hadn't ever given him a second thought. There were so many reasons he and I shouldn't have had a casual relationship, and we understood them completely. So, as we worked together we remained completely professional until the night he exposed his true self.

Enclosed in a very small space even for a submarine, we were completely alone playing cards and surrounded by racks and racks of equipment. He chose the spot, one of my favorite places to hang out alone, because you had to bend and twist to get into this space. Once there, it became a private island — a dry little paradise hunkered down beneath the ocean. That night I made room on my island for him, unaware that a full moon was about to peak over the horizon.

Breaking every single rule I could have recited backward and forward, we sat in silence as our eyes found their way from isolation to companionship. After so many months away from civilization, this night felt as romantic and real as the nights I spent with Jessie in my car, parked high up in the mountains of Montana. He and I stayed in complete silence staring at one another, allowing the silence to communicate for us. When he leaned over to try and kiss me, I was as surprised as you are. We both knew that his unexpected advance had just communicated more than we ever should have.

That was the only night, that singular night, when he put himself at risk with an outward display of emotion while underwater. There wasn't time to have a private conversation, nor was there space to get away and just sit down and talk. We remained completely silent about what had happened and instead he communicated by brushing his arm against mine as he walked by or finding excuses to come up and ask me a navigational question when the submarine was at periscope depth and the control room was completely black

I'm not sure how much time passed until we moved from the darkness of the ocean to the light of day once again, but I found a note tucked into my military uniform the morning we were schedule to pull into port. "Walk out of town, towards the east, past the taxi stand. I will be waiting." With my head spinning faster than the multi-bladed screw that pushed our submarine through the water, I flew through my checklist of required items to secure our ship in port.

Two hours might seem like an eternity for those of you who haven't ever been a part of the military, but on a submarine, two hours is akin to fifteen minutes. Hurry up and wait, and then wait some more. The teamwork required on a submarine requires someone to wait while someone else completes a task or readies a process, so you've always got somebody waiting for something. Today, I was waiting for him. My stomach was aflutter with nervousness as I hunkered down a few hundred feet away from the taxi stand that I knew the other men of the submarine would be using to see the sights. I couldn't risk being seen, as I would be forced to join a group of guys going out for a beer. Heading out on your own, without a buddy, was frowned upon and discouraged at all costs. Since I couldn't tell them I had a buddy coming, as he and I shouldn't have even been talking, I had to hide.

I saw him from a distance and began walking away from him, down the windy road and up a hill. I knew he had seen me and I also knew that with the rest of the submarine on liberty not every sailor would be at a bar getting drunk. I glanced back as I walked and he raised his arm a little higher every time I looked, letting me know that he was following. A mile outside of town I sat down near a tree, halfway up the hill, and waited. I was constantly checking for cars, monitoring how many had passed, looking at the windows in the houses, attempting to see what they could see, and looking for other pedestrians making their own way in the world. He had picked a place of solitude, a road that led to nowhere, which is what my mind surmised when I thought about our situation. Love wasn't possible and probably not even probable, but when you've spent months on end under the ocean the hope of something is better than the possibility of nothing.

My stomach was twisting and turning as I watched him walk up the hill. I had no idea what was about to happen. It had been so long since I had experienced anything but the downbeat of Madonna blasting in my ears as I blew off steam running between the main engines on the submarine to keep in shape, I stood up to greet him with my head bowed. I could feel the heat rising to my face and in my loins – a young man as shy as a sunbeam hidden behind a white billowy cloud. I had never been one to approach another man – it just wasn't my nature. As he walked up and put his arm around me I closed my eyes and exhaled the hunger, fear and sexual tension I had kept bottled up inside for the past two years. Silence rushed in and filled the gap; he took off his hat, turned, and began walking up the hill knowing I would follow.

We looked like two men who had just escaped from prison. Butt white, longer than normal hair, disheveled clothes that had been folded up for the past several months and shoes that seemed more akin to a senior citizen's dance than a rugged hike up a mountainside. He and I stepped alongside one another and got in step, and then laughed when he called out "right, left, right, left." Military men through and through. The danger of our presence together and our private moment was momentarily visible for everyone to see.

Up and up we walked as the land told us a tale of our out-of-shape muscles. I had no idea where we were, but as we rounded the top we were greeted by a flat parcel of land surrounded by rocks. With a view of the city we stood there alone, and together, our arms at our sides, breathing in the view below. My eyes scanned the valley below and the hills around us, wondering just how visible we were. Completely clothed, I felt naked and vulnerable atop that mountain. Missing the moment of what was about to happen before it had even started, he turned to me and grasped my hands, leading them to his chest where he began unbuttoning his shirt.

A love scene in full view for the satellites to capture overhead, the two of us became one. Naked and exposed, it was a first for him and a long awaited reprieve for me. Tender moments, our bodies pressed together, we explored our innermost desires without worries of judgment, consequence or fear. As romantic as a marriage proposal, our lovemaking was tender and strong, submissive and aggressive, and without modesty. With only hours to spare, our military rank and understanding of the rules were tucked away in the clothes that lay crumpled next to us. As the sun winked its last goodbye before it dipped behind the white-capped waves, he and I sat together arm-in-arm with my head resting on his chest. My heart felt like it had been pumped up with a bicycle tire; round, full and ready to burst. We stayed up there over five hours, allowing the day to unfold as naturally as a blooming flower. We knew we had to get back to the black tube of isolation where this moment would be swallowed up by the duties at hand, but we had no other choice. We dressed in silence, staring into each other's eyes, knowing that this moment would never come again. Walking down the hill we began the process of compartmentalizing the moment into our respective history books and as we approached town he walked on ahead, allowing me to linger behind. I caught a taxi halfway down the hill so we wouldn't be caught together.

That was the first and last time he and I said a proper hello, and a solemn goodbye. Circumstances beyond our control forced him off the submarine in a foreign port, and I received a letter several months later telling me that he was getting married. I never heard from him again. I could look him up on Facebook or another social media platform, but for now, I prefer to remember him as he was — a highlight in our submarine deployment together.

The other highlight was the day I finished my qualifications. Nine long months of studying, drawing, discussing and analyzing every single system of the submarine, I finished my written and oral exams a few days before we pulled into La Maddalena, Italy. The crew rarely gathered in a large formation outside of the submarine, especially not in a foreign port. The risk of having the entire crew all standing in one location was a security nightmare, even in 1988, and it was the only time in our six- month deployment where we were all gathered outside in one spot, at one time.

The enlisted men stood side by side, row after row in their working uniforms with their Dixie hats placed in all manners and shapes on their heads. Some curved the tops, others wore them off to one side. Mine was starched and standing at attention on my head. The senior enlisted men stood in front of us, shoulder to shoulder transmitting a message of authority for everyone to see. The real men with the power, the Naval Officers, stood off to one side, their collar devices glistening in the sun, while the Executive Officer stood in the center, waiting for the Commanding Officer to appear.

Commander Connor was our submarine's Captain. All 5'6" of him, a man with a temper hotter than an atomic fireball and a pear-shaped body that dropped over 100 pounds on this six-month deployment. He was all mouth with a voice that knew one volume setting –– LOUD. I felt nothing but distaste for him. My father became an asshole after he drank, but Commander Connor became impossible as soon as his eyes flew open. A screamer, you could routinely hear his nasal voice giving orders at the top of his lungs to anyone and everyone, especially when he didn't get his way. But today, well . . . today was a celebration, so he came up out of the submarine smiling.

We snapped to attention, the Executive Officer saluted the Captain, and he put us at ease. It was a chilly morning in La Maddalena, a rocky coastline with crashing waves and water inlets that glistened in the morning sun. As we stood there it looked like we were all smoking cigarettes as we exhaled and then inhaled the second hand mist from the men standing next to us. I was probably exhaling louder than anyone around me for today I was going to receive my dolphins.

Receiving a set of dolphins feels like being knighted by the Queen of England or receiving a Pulitzer Prize. It is recognition of months of hard work, a key to watching movies in your off-time (instead of studying) and permission to join the submarine as an official member of the crew. Everyone is willing to help you as you work through the qualification process, but you aren't really accepted until you have a set of dolphins pinned on your chest. When Commander Connor raised his hand to receive my qualification letter so he could read it aloud, he called me to the front of the entire crew to stand at attention while he pinned on my dolphins.

The only downside to receiving your dolphins –– or "fish," the nickname for this coveted warfare device-- is the brutal initiation of wearing them. Commander Connor reminded the crew that I was to receive handshakes instead of their fists, which according to tradition, were to be used to drive the dolphins into my chest, "tacking" them to my skin. Hazing was forbidden, at least that's what the policy stated, but we all knew that as soon as the Officers and Senior Enlisted were out of sight, I would receive the congratulatory punches to my left breast causing a bruise the size of a large grapefruit. On cue, the punching began and within a few hours I wore my dolphins, and the grapefruit, with pride.

As the submarine pulled back into Norfolk, I had experienced intimacy in a new way, I had received my dolphins and I was now the primary plotter on the navigation team. I had accomplished the two goals I had set out to conquer and found a new goal in my life — to fall in love with a man.

THE BEGINNING OF THE END
(Age 20)

Back in Norfolk where my submarine had just recently returned from its overseas deployment, the Defense Investigative Service contacted me to let me know that a recommendation for a polygraph by Mr. David Devine (Chief, Polygraph Division) was approved. It stated that the requirements for a polygraph were set forth in DoD Directive 5210.48, DoD 5210-48-R and DIS 20-18-R. Mr. Thomas E. Ewald (Deputy Director of Investigations of the DIS) approved this recommendation. The date was September 9, 1988. With the polygraph looming around every corner, my life started to sag like a worn-out clothesline as I began working twenty-four hour shifts, once again, every three days. Having just completed a six-month deployment, our submarine needed a well-deserved "tune-up" so she moved into dry dock for a three-month break.

During dry dock, the submarine is raised completely out of the water to rest on huge wooden blocks so that engineers can access every part of the submarine to make repairs, install equipment and conduct routine maintenance. It is also the place where the Chief of The Boat put me in charge of spraying sea barnacles off the side of the submarine at night with a high-power hose while perched on top of a cherry picker. That's right — me, in the dead of night, with protective glasses, a helmet and a large rubber suit, wielding a high- powered sprayer in my left hand while my right hand operated a cherry picker that flew me to dizzying heights to clean the encrusted submarine. Even my newly-placed dolphins couldn't get me out of this absolute shit job. I was still one of the most junior ranked men on board, and so I had no choice but to do as I was told.

With lights blazing brighter than a Notre Dame football field in overtime, you could see me waving a wand of water as I moved up and down, along the front, sides and back of our blessed Naval vessel. There were three of us chosen for this coveted assignment, and I was lucky enough to get selected to work the eight-hour night shift. We didn't have iPods back in those days, but I did have protective ear muffs to block out the screaming water as it tore into the submarine's skin, knocking off every form of life that had been clinging to it for the past several years. My hair, teeth, and skin became impacted with unknown sea life and debris I didn't even know existed. They say a bitching sailor is a happy sailor, but in my case, I was just a full blown bitch as I completed that job as fast as I could.

Sooner than I expected, the Defense Investigative Service called me back in for another interview on October 26, 1988 at 10:15 a.m. I was exactly twenty years old, and had been on the submarine just over a year. Upon entering the building, I was greeted by two smiling men, Mr. Lary (from the Defense Investigative Service Headquarters in Washington DC) and Mr. Dillard (Defense Investigative Service Field Office in Norfolk). Mr. Lary explained to me that he was here to administer a polygraph examination while Mr. Dillard sat in the room as a "second set of eyes." Two pairs of eyes . . . were they trying to tell me that Mr. Lary was blind and couldn't see, because I could clearly see what was about to happen –- a crucifixion. With four sets of eyeballs focused squarely on me, I was brought into the polygraph examination room where I squarely refused to take the test. I hadn't spoken to any attorneys and it was difficult for me to research my civil rights while living underwater for six months, but the inner strength I had gained while on the six-month deployment burst forth like a declaration of rape. I flat out told them no. It was a statement that didn't leave room for discussion or bartering. I knew that they couldn't force me to take the polygraph test and all of the aggression I had kept bottled up inside for the past six months came spewing out in the form of defiance. I hadn't been presented any cold hard facts about what they knew and I knew I didn't have to take the polygraph, and so I refused. I remember telling them that unless they had written or eyewitness proof that I was a homosexual; I wasn't going to take the polygraph. They stood there, shocked, like I had just run them over with a car.

Unwilling to let me leave, they asked me to join them in a conference room with a two-way mirror, microphone and table. I sat on one side and they sat on another and for the next four hours and thirty minutes they cajoled and conversed, interrogated and questioned, reasoned and repeated every single word I said. I had no idea if the microphone was on or who was standing behind the two-way mirror, but I knew that without cold hard facts they had nothing. So they pressed and stretched and flattened and steamrolled and ironed me out some more. It took them several hours to work me over to the point that I agreed to write a statement, elaborating on my previous statements, giving them the information that they thought they needed in order to have me discharged from the Navy. All I remember from this interview is the impression that they were not going to let me leave until they had what it is they wanted. And since I refused a polygraph, they chose to double team me instead, eventually wearing me down. The following is the statement I was "asked" to write at the end of my interview:

MY WRITTEN STATEMENT ON 26 OCTOBER 1988:

I, Paul Tripp, do hereby make the following voluntary statement to S/A Lary, who has identified himself as a Special Agent of the Defense Investigative Service. I would like to make this statement to DIS to straighten out my past sexual history which has been questioned. I had lied about my sexual history in prior interviews because I was afraid that the Navy would use it against me and also because it is embarrassing to me. I was also worried that if the information was known aboard the submarine that I would have problems. I would like to tell the truth at this time as I realize that it is a blackmail issue and needs to be addressed. In August 1986 I was in Los Angeles, CA, and lost my job and was low on money so I accepted an offer from Tom G. to stay with him. At one point he made a sexual proposition to me to either have sex with him or get out. I was young and had nowhere to go and gave in to him. The sex amounted to mutual fellatio. This went on for a week and a half until I could get together money to get out of there at which time I flew home. I was very distraught over the matter and it took a long time to get over it. Part of the problem was that I was very confused sexually as a young man because when I was nine years old I was taken sexual advantage of by a cousin who was male. I have since become better adjusted and am convinced that I am not homosexual. This is the only incident of sexual conduct with males that I have had.

Consistent as a Swiss watch, the investigators also filed a report from their perspective as to what happened during the four hour and thirty minute interview. Their statement is as follows:

PURPOSE OF EXAMINATION:

During a DIS investigation, several sources were developed who related that Petty Officer Tripp's activities such as frequenting gay bars, conversations about homosexuality and association with homosexuals, had led several investigators to the conclusion that Petty Officer Tripp was engaging in homosexual activities. Petty Officer Tripp denied that he had ever engaged in any sexual activity with another male, and agreed to submit to a polygraph examination to confirm his denial.

DETAILS:

On 26 October 1988, Seaman Tripp presented himself for an interview, but advised that he was not willing to undergo polygraph testing. However, Tripp did agree to be interviewed. During the initial stages of the interview, Seaman Tripp continued to deny any sexual contact with a male. After a brief period, Seaman Tripp advised that the reason he had sexual identity questions about himself was that when he was age nine he and an older cousin performed mutual fellatio on each other on two separate occasions. Tripp advised that he has numerous homosexual friends from his work in theater and other activities. Tripp also advised that in high school he had engaged in mutual masturbation with another male after a high school dance. Eventually, Tripp admitted that while in Los Angeles, Aug 1986, he moved in with Tom G., a homosexual, who insisted that Tripp engage in sexual activity in exchange for residing there. Tripp stated that for a period of about one and a half weeks he engaged in mutual fellatio with Tom until Tripp saved enough money to buy a plane ticket to return home. Tripp denied that he had sexual activity with other males. Seaman Tripp advised that for fear of AIDS he has not engaged in any sexual activity for one and a half years. Tripp advised that he had concealed this activity mentioned from DIS because he was afraid the Navy would use it against him, that DIS would hold prior false statements against him and that if his prior sexual activities became common knowledge aboard his submarine, he would be subjected to ridicule. Tripp advised that he felt a need for counseling in regards to his sexual activity at age nine because it still gave him doubts about himself, but that he had never had any counseling in regards to this matter. Tripp advised that the only person whom he knew who was aware of this prior sexual activity and who was possibly in a position to blackmail him was Tom G. and the cousin, whom Tripp declined to identify. A written statement was obtained.

There it was, out on the table, the missing piece to the puzzle that caused them to stop searching. What they wanted, from the very beginning, was for me to admit that I had experienced intercourse with another man, and up until this fateful day, I had denied this accusation. I had refused to admit it, I had challenged them to find proof, and I had repeated over and over and over again that I had not had any type of homosexual encounter, thought or action -- until today.

In retrospect, I believe I relented because I was sick of the investigations, sick of the threats that hung over my head and sick and tired of being called into the investigators' office when I least expected it to try and explain myself. I knew they didn't have absolute proof that I was a homosexual because I had doubted that I would ever live an openly gay life, even to myself. A young man with same-sex attraction but repulsed by the gay lifestyle, I still allowed myself the mental escape that there might be another way to live. Until October 28, 1988, I refused to admit to anyone in a position of authority that I had ever experienced any type of homosexual sex. This final investigation sucked the life right out of me, and without a hope of leaving the room until I gave them some kind of statement, I told them what I thought would get them off my back, but hopefully not enough to have my security clearance taken away or get me kicked out of the Navy for lying.

By admitting that I had experienced homosexual sex before entering the military, and not admitting this to the recruiter who interviewed me before I came into the Navy, put me in a precarious position of having fraudulently enlisted. The Navy could have me brought up on charges for giving false information and discharged me within weeks, but I was still unsure about what information could be shared between my security clearance investigation and the Captain of my submarine.

With my future uncertain, I left the interview in silence.

ESCAPE

(Age 21)

Why did I have to come to terms with my sexuality through a series of interviews, threats and an intense investigation? A child of God since the eighth grade, I knew I had feelings for men, but I didn't want to lead a gay lifestyle in the way I understood it to exist in 1988. I wasn't sure if I could change my sexuality. I had prayed to God to give me the wisdom of his words so that I could understand my situation and, in the interim, I was like every other young adult I knew — I went out to blow off steam both upstairs and down. There wasn't one other person I knew who was forced to talk about what they did in the bedroom to a roomful of men and then sign a piece of paper denying their truth.

Men, their penises and the fear surrounding sexuality are such complicated issues. I knew of two men with Top Secret clearances who had committed adultery during our most recent six-month deployment, but they weren't being dragged through the court of judgment like I was. For the record, adultery can be processed as a violation of the Uniform Code of Military Justice (Article 134), punishable up to a discharge.

Another man got crabs from a hooker in a foreign port and we were all forced to strip our beds, wash our clothing and put on a slimy liquid to kill the bugs, and what happened to him? Nothing. Heterosexual sex was fine, and it didn't matter if you fucked her doggy style, upside down, with a wedding ring or not, nobody was going to call you on the carpet and take away your security clearance. I however made a comment that caused some people to think I was a homosexual and for the past two years I had suffered the wrath of a team of investigators who didn't give up until they made me admit that I had indeed, sucked dick.

With a new chip on my shoulder, the routine of work regained its cadence and I remained silent about my October 26, 1988 interview. I should have told the Navigator, the Executive Officer or requested a face-to-face interview with the Commanding Officer in an attempt to stop the unstoppable damage before it hit my life and shattered it to pieces, but instead, I stayed silent. I suppose my pride got in the way, for I wasn't going to cut my life open for a new set of bystanders and let all of my diseased organs fall onto the floor in front of them so that they could make an assessment on my character. I had experienced enough judgment from my parents, the three bullies in grade school, the South American Exchange Student Coordinator and now the investigators. I became resolutely silent. A shell of anger built up around me, spurring me to work harder than I ever had.

Driven by a mixture of anger and shame, I churned out work faster and better than anyone had ever seen. If my peers stayed until 6 p.m., I stayed until 8 p.m. If they worked on one project and had a completion date in five days, I worked on three projects and finished them in four days. I volunteered for every assignment, went to additional training, and worked on my advancement exams with a feverish dedication. I was going to be the best sailor anyone had ever seen, all I needed was time. I knew the clock was ticking on my potential military discharge back to Montana.

October 1988 to April 1989, the months flew by without a word from anyone. I didn't have a clue why it was taking them so long to process me out of the Navy on the basis of a fraudulent enlistment, but I never spoke it aloud. With my twenty-first birthday igniting all the candles on my cake, I found myself on vacation in Montana, by choice, hitting the bars in a drunken state. My parents wanted to know every last detail and so I told them the half-truths I had become so skilled at baking in my mental oven. The Navy was great, I had a ton of friends, I was getting promoted and I was on the fast track for something great. As I left Montana to head back to Virginia I was once again forced to look at the lies that formed jagged cracks down the middle of my life.

May of 1989 the submarine headed down to Fort Lauderdale, Florida to conduct some drills, and to give the crew a well-deserved rest. Four days in Fort Lauderdale and I was twenty-one years old. I had my dolphins so I didn't have to spend my free time studying, and I was fortunate enough to get assigned duty on the first night, which meant that I had two whole days free. It was the first time I was able to escape the rigors of submarine life in a port and truly experience freedom. I wasn't sure what I was looking for, but I sure as hell wasn't going to start looking by staying on the submarine.

A few guys from my division had asked me to go out and grab a beer, but I just couldn't muster the strength. Another drunken night looking at girls' tits talking about work in a bar filled with horny submariners, my mind cracked at the invitation. I told everyone I was going to see family down in Miami and would be back in the morning. I had no idea where Miami was nor did I have a hotel room, but I knew I could sleep in the car if my plans didn't work out. I just wanted out. I got off the submarine and into a rental car as fast as I could.

I ended up at a bar called the Copa Cabana. Without Google, an iPhone or a GPS navigation system, I have no idea how I found that bar and no idea how I managed to navigate my way towards that starry-filled night, but there I was. A smoky bar, filled with men, 1989, twenty-one, a real ID. I had just stepped inside when a guy offered to buy me a drink and by the time I got back from the bathroom, another guy offered the same. It looked like I had found a treasure of booty, and I couldn't have been happier.

I sat down, opened up a pack of smokes, ordered a drink and took a hit of both at the same time. Whiskey chasing down the sweet taste of Marlboro reds, I truly was the poster boy for Montana. I sat there for a few hours, drinking, looking, drinking, and smoking. This bar could have been on the edge of a crumbling cliff and I wouldn't have moved. Gay. Free. No pretense, no judgment, no nothing. Just the sound of the music, the taste of deliciousness and the sweet smell of cigarette smoke. Freedom.

At 9 p.m. the music started and I hit the dance floor. The only way I stayed in shape on the submarine was running in place for thirty minutes a day between the main engines, always to dance music, so I just let myself go when I stepped out to Madonna's raspy tone. The lone crazy dancer — you've seen them, right? It's kind of like watching a car crash. Part of you wants to gasp and turn away and the other part of you can't stop staring. But, when you're trapped underwater for 72+ days at a time, you dance like no-one is watching, you sing like no-one is listening, and you say anything you damn well please. It was the best feeling of the night, that and Paulo's first kiss.

Paulo. Time has erased the memory of how I met him or the drive back to his place, but the rest of the night I cannot forget. A 6'3" Brazilian with dark hair, dark eyes, beautiful big hands, and lips as soft as a chinchilla fur coat. As I parked the car I remember him leaning over to run his hands through my hair. He got out and we walked to the beach and just stood there, his hand in mine. The swoosh of the ocean and the sparkle of the stars were enough conversation for both of us. We stood there for a good forty-five minutes, in silence, looking at one another, gazing up at the stars and listening to the ocean. I didn't feel a need to ask him one single question as he had already given me all the answers.

Submarine life is lonely. Encapsulated in a tube that sinks beneath the ocean for minutes that turn to hours, hours that turn into days and days that turn into months – it's a cold existence with no touch, no embrace, no warm words of encouragement, and some days no warm water. A barren existence. No milk, no vegetables, no sunlight — just a floating steel floor, electronic equipment and a nuclear reactor. I used to joke that we weren't there to serve the Navy; we were there to serve the submarine. She was in control, and we just pushed her buttons to keep her happy. An unforgiving mistress, she could take our lives without a moment's notice.

As Paulo and I stood at the water's edge, I mentally recorded that moment and put it in my own time capsule to play on those quiet nights when only whales were making noise. He led me from the water and into his house, just a few feet away. He stood there, looking at me, smiling, with the silence speaking softly in our ears. He took my head in his hands and pulled me close to his chest, allowing me to rest like the weary traveler I was.

The night turned slowly into early morning and we remained, hand in hand, lips on lips, side by side. He allowed me to exhale, somehow understanding my need to say everything at once, and nothing at all. Our arms reached above our heads, fingers moving in and out trying to find the perfect connection. Giggles, kisses, and a soft caress across the face… All I ever found out was that he was from Brazil.

We never went to sleep and we never got naked. As I finally got up to leave, I started to cry, years of hurt escaping from my soul. Paulo took off his ring and slipped it on my finger. A keepsake, he said. Don't ever forget this night. I wondered if I ever would.

Rental car returned and back on the submarine, I felt as though a part of me had come alive, and then died a sudden death. In the dark space of the navigation area I shed many tears over Paulo. A man I didn't know, a man I barely spoke to, and a man whose ring I was wearing. He's held a place in my memory for twenty-three years now. Paulo. It was a pleasure meeting you.

COMMANDER BOROX
(Age 21 – 22)

As we dove beneath the ocean with Fort Lauderdale disappearing from view, our next two stops were Puerto Rico and then over to St. Croix, Virgin Islands. Our Commanding Officer, Commander Connor, was getting ready to turn over the submarine to a new Commanding Officer, Commander Borox. We met him in Puerto Rico, all 6'3" of him, with brown silent eyes, shaky hands and a trim build. Nice enough, he was all business and toured the different departments of the submarine with precision. On time and with a notebook in hand, it was clear that this man was nothing if not punctual. My only hope was that he wouldn't punch our glass plotters like Commander Connor, and please Lord, no screaming.

It is a rare event when the submarine goes out to sea and receives permission to visit ports for crew rest and relaxation. It is even rarer still when the submarine surfaces like a cork bobbing in a bathtub, so the crew can have a "swim call." That's right, we got to use the submarine as our diving board as we jumped in cannonball, head first, swan dive and sideways, all in the name of fun. With the Caribbean ocean as clear as a water-filled glass, we were allowed one hour of blissful uninterrupted swimming all around the front part of the submarine. Wet, relaxed and sun kissed, we submerged once again and headed home to Norfolk for the official Change of Command ceremony, in which Commander Borox would become our new Commanding Officer.

With the pomp and circumstance of Navy tradition complete, our submarine began a new set of operational missions under the helm of our new Commander and we began preparing for a North Atlantic deployment where we'd spend three months traversing the ice of the northern Atlantic seas while participating in scheduled exercises with other US Naval vessels. The crew was scheduled for a review of each member's security clearance, standard practice for a lengthy deployment, and I knew exactly what that meant for me –– more security clearance trouble.

Within weeks of Commander Borox taking the helm as the Commanding Officer, I was informed that the Defense Investigative Service had denied my eligibility for a Top Secret clearance. Faced with a difficult situation, Commander Borox called me to his stateroom for a meeting with the Executive Officer, Navigator and the good Commander. I was an E-4, the ship's primary plotter, and one of the best members of the navigation team. Over the next hour, I was peppered with questions about why I was denied my security clearance and the events surrounding my case. It was a humiliating experience and I stated as little as possible, allowing my superior officers to lead the discussion. I knew they had read my case file, the reports filed by the Defense Investigative Service and all of the comments and sworn statements by each side. The investigator's position was clear, I had lied about my homosexual experiences that occurred prior to my entrance into the Navy, and the Defense Investigative Service had denied my TS/SCI security clearance. Without a clearance, I would be unable to deploy with the submarine, putting my ability to serve the Navy at risk. Commander Borox, recognizing my dilemma, came to a different conclusion.

Oprah has a saying that when someone shows you who they are, believe them. I had been showing every single person possible that I had capabilities beyond my rank, was willing to work harder than anyone else and would do whatever it took to continue to promote. That had been my attitude since my last fatal investigative interview and everyone on the ship had taken notice. It was the first time I understood the lesson that if your boss looks good, you will also, and I couldn't have been happier. Commander Borox decided to give me an interim Top Secret clearance so I could join the ship and deploy to the Northern Atlantic Region. Ultimately I don't know what swayed his decision, but it was a decision that changed the course of my life and breathed new hope into my desire to stay in the Navy to complete my twenty-year career.

With an interim Top Secret clearance granted by Commander Borox, the submarine began its three-month deployment to Holy Lock and Rosyth in Scotland, Haakonsvern, Norway and Zeebrugge, Belgium -- a fascinating tour of the world. We stayed underwater for close to sixty days, but the places we saw were well worth the sacrifice. I toured Haakonsvern with my tennis shoes and Walkman, running through neighborhoods that were built into cliffs overlooking the ocean. Scotland allowed me the opportunity to visit Edinburgh and Inverkeithing, while Belgium took me to Brugge, Antwerp, Brussels, Knokke and Ghent. Gent is where I learned about Van Gogh and bought my first umbrella, which I still have to this day. That umbrella and I slept together all the way back to America, the only thing I slept with for quite some time.

As 1990 rounded out its final months, I found myself contemplating re-enlistment into the Navy for six more years or getting out. Not knowing anything about the circumstances surrounding my security clearance, the pressure from the senior enlisted men on board my submarine to re-enlist was strong. I was stopped once or twice a day and given a "talking to" on how great a career in the Navy would be. The officers, on the other hand, who had full knowledge of my entire security investigation told me that I should get out and go to college full time. I remember one conversation in particular where the Navigator told me that it would be impossible to work full-time and go to school full-time. He told me that if I really wanted a college education, I should get out. The question was, get out to where?

We had been underwater for so many months that I wasn't afforded time to research colleges. We didn't have anything like internet accessibility on the submarine, so in order to apply and correspond I was limited to a library and a mailing address that was linked to a moving vessel whose mail came weeks, if not months, late. I had been too focused on the tasks at hand to think about my future, and with a decision now on my doorstep I was less prepared than ever before to leave the Navy.

Although I had been denied a Top Secret/SCI clearance, Commander Borox had granted me an interim clearance and never made mention of a possible discharge from the Navy based upon the findings of the security clearance investigation. A young sailor, I failed to understand the complexities of how I might need a security clearance in the future, or how the facts of my security clearance investigation could continue to cause me trouble. Instead, I was given the promise of a re-enlistment bonus of $12,000 and a choice assignment in San Diego. With the approval from Commander Borox, I re-enlisted in the Navy for six more years with orders to report to Submarine Group Five in San Diego as an operational scheduler in January 1991. The Navy had not taken any action on my possible fraudulent enlistment discharge, so as I signed the papers to re-enlist, I keep my mouth closed as well. Commander Borox shook my hand; I took the check, and assumed that everything related to my clearance had been resolved.

What I didn't know at the time is that the issue of my security clearance would put my San Diego job in jeopardy and begin the process of discharging me out of the Navy.

SAN DIEGO

(Age 22 – 23)

I left the USS CINCINNATI SSN-693 on December 17, 1990, flew home to Montana for Christmas, bought my mom's white Toyota Camry, and with a song in my heart and exhausted legs from skiing during my Christmas break, I made a break for San Diego and reported for work as an operational scheduler.

An operational scheduler is akin to an underwater traffic controller. Three men schedule the activities of all the submarines moving in and out of San Diego. It wasn't a job for the weak hearted. We worked in three-week shifts. One week I wrote the schedule, the next week I reviewed the schedule, made changes and got the schedule approved, and the third week I was "active" with my schedule and on-call twenty-four hours a day for the next seven days. Once the active week ended, I started the process from the beginning; writing the schedule that would go active in exactly two weeks. It sounds easy, right? Right.

It took me three months to learn the job. I was as nervous as a cat on a hot tin roof as I prepared my first operational schedule. This submarine leaving at this time, that submarine surfacing at that time, two submarines conducting an exercise off the coast with different depth separation schemes, another submarine needing to transit on the surface above all of them — oh my Lord — and I had to know every answer to every single question. When the phone rang at night, I was the person they called to come in and fix the problem, and once I had a solution I had to call my boss to get it approved. It was a job which required the memory of an elephant and the speed of a jackrabbit.

On May 16, 1991, three months and sixteen days after I started my three-year stint as an underwater traffic controller, my boss informed me that my new Command, Submarine Group Five, had received a naval message concerning my security clearance. It read:

From: Director, Department of the Navy Central Adjudication Facility
To: Commander, Submarine Group Five, 137 Sylvester Road San Diego, CA 92106
Subject: QM2 PAUL BRIAN TRIPP, USN
Reference: (a) OPNAVINST 5510.1H
        (b) OPNAVNOTE 5510 Serial 09N/9U651172 of 12 May 1989
Enclosure: (1) DIS Special Background Investigation 16 November 1988

1. Enclosure (1) has been reviewed in accordance with references (a) and (b) and is forwarded for your action. It contains information that may have a bearing on the subject's security eligibility.

2. **The enclosed information provides indications of possible behavior, mental or emotional condition, or illness which could cause a defect in judgment or reliability. Request, therefore, that you obtain a current mental health evaluation conducted by a US government-employed or contract psychiatrist (board certified or board eligible) or licensed clinical psychologist in accordance with the above references.** This evaluation is needed to aid this command in the determination of subject's eligibility for access to highly sensitive, classified defense information.

3. Provide a copy of this letter and the enclosure to the examining psychiatrist/psychologist with a caution that the specific information developed from sources other than the subject should not be discussed with the individual in such a manner as to disclose the identity of these sources, thus undermining their mutual relationship, as well as violating a commitment of confidentiality. **The results of the evaluation should include a diagnosis and prognosis of the subject's condition, if any, and be of sufficient scope to enable the examiner to state whether the subject is under any prescribed medication and whether the condition represents a possible defect in judgment, reliability, or stability, with due regard to the transient or continuing effect of the condition.** It should also address the subject's ability to withstand pressure or coercion if threatened with exposure of the mental or emotional condition.

4. Please return the enclosure with the mental health evaluation results in 60 days of the date of this letter. Also, request you provide any additional information which may have a bearing on the subject's security eligibility (e.g., incident reports, arrest records, etc.). Your expeditious action and response will be greatly appreciated in view of the importance of this matter.

Signed – B. Sullivan, By direction

So let me break this down for you. I left my old job with two personal awards, unheard of for someone of my rank, and had just been approved to re-enlist into the Navy for six more years. Within four months of arriving on a new job, a letter arrives telling my new boss that I need a psychiatric evaluation within the next sixty days to determine if I have a mental illness, to see if I can withstand pressure or coercion and, oh yeah, don't give the subject all of the facts about who said what to whom because we don't want him to know anything other than what we tell him. If all of that wasn't enough, Enclosure (1) was some type of correspondence that the Defense Investigative Service had written to my new boss that I wasn't given a copy of. For the record, I still haven't seen a copy of this correspondence.

Now let's just say you hire an employee, train him and he is now responsible for the lives of hundreds of people. A few days after you determine that he is qualified to work without supervision, a letter comes from an investigating agency that states he needs a psychiatric evaluation. Wouldn't you want to pull him out of his job, put him on a dead-end assignment and then let him go as quickly as is ethically allowed? There are enough whack jobs, lazy people, folks with hidden agendas and checkered pasts to write ten novels –- and I was now squarely in that category. I was too new in my job to allow my work ethic to speak for me, so instead, I was forced to speak up and explain the entire situation to a new set of people, all over again.

Worse than a herpes outbreak, this ongoing investigation was a gift that forced me to pull down my pants and stand butt naked explaining every awkward mole and pimple of my past. Denigrated and feeling worse about myself than I ever had before, the message from the Defense Investigative Service hit me squarely in the heart of ambition, self-doubt and self-esteem. I felt like a completely worthless piece of shit, all because of a single comment I made four years earlier. I will say it again — why did my sexual preference matter so much? The Navy said blackmail, and I said bullshit. If I hadn't given in to the pit bulls who forced me to go through several verbal investigations, how did they think I was going to respond to a blackmail threat? My answer had always been, and remains, a resolute "fuck you" when it comes to talking about my sexual preference at work. But, there I was, forced to re-open my past once more to explain what I understood to be the difficulties surrounding my ability to obtain a TS/SCI security clearance.

Nine days later my world came crashing down on me. The date was May 25, 1991 and I was twenty-three years old. It was a hot day in San Diego, one of those blue sky you can see forever kind of days. I remember it so well because I had just come in from a ten mile run with one of my co-workers, and we were sitting down to eat lunch when the phone rang. I was told that Lieutenant Hellen, the administrative officer for Submarine Group Five wanted to see me in his office. I ticked down the list of all the things that could have caused me to be called up to the Admiral's secretary; not completing my required reading, not submitting my completed study guides for my next promotion, disrespect to a senior officer, not answering my phone when work called. Hard as I tried, I couldn't come up with one single thing that would have caused me to be called into Mr. Hellen's office, which sat high up on the hill, in a sterile hallway, right outside the Admiral's office.

As I walked in and sat down, I could tell that something was terribly wrong. Lieutenant Hellen wasn't the friendliest of officers. A tall man with a rugged chin, the kind of guy you would see at a sport's bar ogling the waitresses' tits while slamming back a beer watching the big game on TV. The kind of guy who left his wife at home to take care of the kids, because it was her job and his job was to go to work and then do whatever suited his fancy on the weekends because he had the penis and she didn't. He was that kind of guy. He played by the rules, his rules, and had no regard for anyone without a collar device that didn't outrank his.

After reading the document that the Defensive Investigative Service had included in the message on May 16, 1991, Lieutenant Hellen "regretted to inform me" that he was going to start the paperwork to administratively separate me from the Navy due to the fact that I had falsified my enlistment documents by stating I had never had a homosexual encounter.

The last words he spoke to me were, "Petty Officer Tripp, if you feel suicidal, go see the Chaplain. Now, you're dismissed."

With the chaplain gone for the day, I was sent to the Navy "doctor," who was really a glorified nurse. He sat in his chair and asked me if I had thought about killing myself, if I had a plan and if I was feeling suicidal. I had just received the news that I was being kicked out of the Navy for admitting that I had two homosexual encounters before I joined, I would have to repay the $12,000 re-enlistment bonus and would be sent back to Montana. Was I feeling suicidal? No, actually, I was feeling homicidal by the stupid questions he kept asking me. The Navy had a habit of treating its sailors only as smart as the rank on their sleeves, and as a second class Petty Officer I was in the middle rank for enlisted men, so that meant I was still required to be treated like a third grader. I left the "doctor's" office, got in my car and headed home.

The message that the Navy was sending me was that my sexuality mattered more than hard work and dedication. Never mind that I wasn't currently having any kind of sex as I was working nine hours a day and attending college five nights a week. I had never been accused of being gay at work, had never mentioned my sexuality in the workplace, nor did I partake in the homoerotic jokes that my heterosexual counterparts peppered throughout the office. I was a model sailor who had recently been nominated as "Sailor of the Quarter," but the Navy was willing to discharge me because of two incidents that took place prior to entering the military.

I went home furious. Fuck suicidal. The only person I wanted to kill was the nameless motherfucker who made up these rules. I could understand if I had setup a glory hole in the bathroom or made overt gestures towards my co-workers, but none of that had happened. Fuck suicidal.

THE FIGHT

(Age 23)

My father subscribes to the philosophy that strength comes in the form of two fists, a concept even the school bully, David, couldn't beat into me. A fighter I was, but not in the way my dad believed. As I got up the next morning I knew I had no choice but to fight. And fight is exactly what I did.

One of the things I came to understand and appreciate about the Navy is that regardless of your rank, you can always ask for, and typically be granted, an audience with the highest supervisor in your work place. The Navy doesn't have a designated Human Resource department where its employees can file complaints to a dedicated staff who will investigate and answer them. Instead, if you need to file a complaint or speak to a senior officer, you are required to submit a piece of paperwork asking to speak to that respective officer. As the paperwork travels up your chain of command, you are required to speak to every single person who signs the document, giving them the facts of your case. The other option, which pisses everyone off to no end, is to knock on the door of the Senior Officer you want to speak with and request a private audience. Having just been told by LT Hellen that I was going to be administratively separated from the Navy, I didn't have the time or the stomach to wait two weeks for a piece of paperwork to get approved. I was beyond the point where I felt like I needed to bare my soul to every single man within my chain of command. If the Navy was going to kick me out, I was going to do everything possible to get the attention of the most senior officer I could speak with. So, the very next morning I got up and knocked on the door of Captain Chotvacs, the Chief of Staff for Submarine Group Five.

Captain Chotvacs stood about 5'4" with a black handlebar moustache and a stare that scared death away. He told me to be seated, which I did after he sat down, and then I opened myself up like a coke bottle waiting to explode and spewed every last detail of my investigation all over his office. He sat there with a straight face, barely blinked, didn't take notes, and didn't ask me one question. He listened, nodded, listened and nodded. When I was done, he rose from his desk, told me that he would not stop my administrative separation from the Navy, but would use his authority to have me scheduled for a psychological examination as quickly as possible. He told me that the results of the examination would be the determining factor if he processed me for administrative separation or allowed me to stay in. With a handshake, he opened up his office door and told me to get back to work.

That was as good as it was going to get, and I left his office shaking as this was the first time I had taken the initiative to speak every detail aloud. Honest, straightforward and without a single word of judgment, he told me what I could expect. My entire career would hinge on the findings of one person –- a Navy psychologist. For the next eleven days I was an absolute wreck. I couldn't call my family, for they had no idea what was going on. I had one friend in the area, a dentist named Mark Cage, but I couldn't open up to him because I was so embarrassed by what I perceived to be character assassinations framed as an investigation to ensure that the Navy was employing the right people. I called my old friend, Chuck, in Virginia to share my news, but he had gotten out of the Air Force and told me that it would be a blessing if the same thing happened to me. I didn't want to get kicked out. I had never been kicked out of anything in my life, and if I were going to leave the Navy, it was going to be on my terms.

June 16, 1991, twenty-three years of age, is the day my life hung in the balance. Montana had less appeal to me than when I left, and if I were to be kicked out for fraudulent enlistment, I would lose the GI Bill, which was currently paying for my college education. Separation from the Navy meant I'd have to go back home and work retail until I saved up enough money to go back to school.

I didn't tell any of my enlisted co-workers what was going on. I tried in every single way possible to keep this problem quiet –- very quiet –- and told the guys in my office that I had a medical appointment for my knee. My direct supervisor, Commander Knight, knew why I wasn't at work, but he gave nothing away. He shook my hand as I readied to leave, patted me on the shoulder, and told me to give the doctor hell. Commander Knight was a class act — no questions, no comments and no advice — he treated me as if I were his best sailor.

I arrived at the office of LCDR E.C. Calix, a staff psychologist, a few minutes before my appointment. A younger guy, he didn't give me any impression that he cared about me one way or the other. He seemed like he was a bit bored by his work and was just trying to make it through the day so he could go home and relax. He asked me to sit down, he made a comment about the weather, and then he began with his questions. No fanfare, no accusatory tone, I felt like I was talking to a person who was a thousand miles away worrying about the problems in his own life. Question, answer, question, answer. I was so used to the Defense Investigators' techniques of accusations and questions and then more accusations, the tenor of the psychologist caught me off guard. He interviewed me for just over an hour, thanked me, walked me to the door and told me to enjoy the rest of my day. With no thunder or lightning, I wondered if he had heard a word I said.

I left the building not knowing what LCDR Calix was going to write, and to be completely honest, I was scared out of my mind. I also did not care. On some level I knew that I had spoken my truth, that my sexuality was not a factor in my ability to serve in the military. On the other hand I knew I had violated the same code of conduct that I held so near and dear to my heart. I loved the structure of the military for it had allowed me to understand the boundaries and then soar to the highest levels of performance and competence. Growing up in an alcoholic home, I was never sure where the beginning was or where on the path I would hit a landmine and have the evening explode in front of me. The Navy was the perfect place for me, and I hoped I had convinced LCDR Calix that I didn't want to be separated against my will. For the record, I vehemently denied any homosexual tendencies or attraction. Like Peter in the Bible, I had finally denied, denied and denied my authentic self.

It took three days for Captain Chotvacs to call me into his office. By that point, I was ready to eat a hairball in order to salvage my career. On his doorstep one more time, I realized that this was a moment of truth. He told me to sit down, and slid the following report (modified due to length) for me to read:

LCDR CALIX'S MENTAL STATUS EXAM SUMMARY:

Fully oriented, reluctantly cooperative young man was occasionally hostile to questions as he does not feel he has a mental disorder. Mood was anxious, occasionally hostile, with ranging affect. Speech was clear, normal in rate and tone. There were no signs of psychosis, affective disorder or disabling neurosis. Judgment and insight were adequate. Patient sometimes seemed excitable and dramatic in stating "his case" as it were. There were no signs of homicidal or suicidal ideations or plan. Patient is fit for full duty; no mental disorders. It cannot be reliably established that member either is or isn't a homosexual (he certainly denies this) and homosexuality is not listed as a mental disorder in DSM-III. It is up to Submarine Group Five or other sources to determine the presence or absence of this (homosexuality). There is not sufficient evidence to indicate that QM2 Tripp would be a security risk whatever his sexual orientation. However, I am unclear as to why he did not submit to a polygraph in 1988. QM2 Tripp appears sincere in his commitment to the Navy and his outstanding record is testimony to this.

LCDR CALIX WENT ON IN HIS REPORT TO STATE:

He empathetically denied any homosexual behavior or tendencies. He seemed hostile to the whole examination process but revealed he had "nothing to hide." He also stated that this is "the last time" he would submit himself to this type of investigation. QM2 Tripp denied being susceptible to blackmail or other acts of coercion while stating that the Navy's "witch hunts" against homosexuals was quite unnecessary. He stated that they should be concerned more with "The Walkers" and the Marines in the Embassy in Russia. He also stated that he had refused the polygraph test in 1988 because he did not feel it was necessary and questioned its accuracy. [. . .] He strongly desires to remain in the Naval Service and pointed to his 4.0 record and Navy Achievement Medals as proof of his exemplary record. QM2 Tripp has the goal of becoming a commissioned officer, but fears this investigation may hinder that. He says he will obtain a lawyer if necessary.

Captain Chotvacs waited for me to finish reading the entire report (over four pages long), and when I looked up he was sitting in his chair with his hands folded, staring a hole in me. Then the questions began.

RESOLUTION
(Age 23)

Captain Chotvacs didn't suffer fools lightly. He knew that when he saw smoke billowing from above, a raging fire was burning down below. Crusty as a dried out piece of bread, I doubted he still kept his fire lit, but I knew sitting across from him that he knew what I knew. He was the perfect contradiction of a salty Naval Officer. A rule follower who enforced the Uniform Code of Military Justice with a steel fist, and yet allowed the nuances of my situation to be defined by a psychologist's report while he made good on his promise to write to the Navy Central Adjudication Facility asking that my clearance be re-instated. He didn't flat out ask me if I was a homosexual because to him the psychologist already told him that answer –– it couldn't be determined. He was now the second Naval Officer (Commander Borox was the first) who looked my situation directly in the face and decided that it wasn't definitive enough to terminate my employment.

Although Commander Borox was the first Naval Officer who allowed me to serve due to my proven job performance, Captain Chotvacs was the man who saved the day. Instead of judging without facts, he allowed the process to unfold in due course, and when the answer came down from the psychologist, he accepted the findings as fact and chose not to entertain any more investigative foolishness. He proceeded with pointy-knife sharpness; writing messages, clarifying facts and working to get my case favorably adjudicated. As far as Captain Chotvacs was concerned, my case was no longer a topic of conversation to be re-opened and torn apart for review.

I'm not sure how anyone can continue to review the argument against the biological hard wiring of sexual orientation. After years of investigations I ask you to think about the hypothesis that if homosexuality is indeed a choice, why wouldn't I have chosen to be straight? Do you believe that I really wanted to be interrogated for hours on end, having to explain myself to every single person who came in contact with the details of my investigation? Every single time I was hauled in to the investigators' offices, the office of Commander Borox and now Captain Chotvacs was a lesson in humiliation. If I had a choice, I would have chosen not to be gay or have homosexual feelings towards men, but the truth –- my truth –- and the truth of every other homosexual person on this planet is that homosexual desires are not a choice. Who in their right mind would endure years of mental torture? Certainly not me. I would have given anything to make this situation disappear, to the point of lying repeatedly about my homosexual tendencies.

I lied over and over and over again so I could keep my job. I knew that the lies tore at the fiber of my being, for I prided myself on hard work and honesty, but I wasn't going to give in just to let the Navy kick me out. I worked hard, I loved the military, and my sexual orientation was not going to get the best of me. Again, I ask you -- how in the world can you read this story and still wonder if homosexual desires are biologically hard-wired or a choice. Think about it.

In July 1991, with the psychologist's report complete, Captain Chotvacs drafted and signed the following message to the Navy Central Adjudication Facility, the people who would ultimately decide the fate of the second part of my security clearance, the Special Compartmented Information (SCI) portion:

From: Commander Submarine Group Five
To: Director, Department of the Navy Central Adjudication Facility
Subject: QM2 (SS) PAUL BRIAN TRIPP, USN
Reference: (a) Department of the Navy Central Adjudication Facility
        Message of 16 May 91
    (b) Phone conversation between COMSUBGRU FIVE
        and USS CINCINNATI
    (c) Military Personnel Manual 3630400
Enclosure: (1) Report of psychological evaluation SF 600 of 06 Jun
        1991

1. In response to reference (a), enclosure (1) is provided. The clinical psychologist has found subject fit for full duty and that there is insufficient evidence to support that subject is a security risk.

2. The psychologist, this command, and subject's previous command as confirmed by reference (b), all agree that there is no behavior, mental or emotional condition, or illness which could cause a defect in judgment or reliability, nor does subject's history preclude his ability to safeguard classified information. Reference (b) further re-enforces the foregoing in that USS CINCINNATI, having full knowledge of the initial Defense Investigative Service report (enclosure (1) to reference (a)), favorably adjudicated subject's security clearance, continued his participation in the Personnel Reliability Program (PRP) and re-enlisted him in December 1990.

3. The incidents described in enclosure (1) occurred prior to subject's enlistment. The first incident occurred at age nine and was a non-consequential experience typical in childhood development. The second occurred just prior to subject's initial enlistment and was a result of coercion and immature judgment caused by situational vulnerability in not being able to meet basic living expenses. While statements made by character references do speculate that subject may be homosexual, the speculations are not supported by fact, nor do they cite any witnessed genuine homosexual acts by or with subject. While a positive statement cannot be made as to subject's sexual preference, and there is no other evidence other than speculations to suggest that subject is homosexual.

4. Enclosure (1) identifies subject's hostility and frustration regarding the continual resurfacing of this issue. Subject's reaction is understandable and acceptable. By the actions taken by USS CINCINNATI, subject understood that this issue was put to rest. He is anxious to get this issue resolved once and for all so that he can continue his Navy career, as a quartermaster, and in the submarine service.

5. Due to subject's admissions to DIS investigators, in depth review by USS CINCINNATI and this command, and because the issue is now a matter of record, it is believed that vulnerability to blackmail or coercion is slight.

6. It is strongly recommended that this case be favorably and quickly adjudicated, and that official headquarters' records be sufficiently documented to preclude subsequent routine investigative efforts from unduly resurfacing this issue.

7. Administrative separation processing mandated by reference (c) will be addressed by separate correspondence to the Chief of Naval Personnel following your adjudication of the case. Every effort will be made to retain subject in the Navy, in his present status.

8. Interim TOP SECRET access will continue unless otherwise directed.

Signed, C.J. CHOTVACS – Chief of Staff

A watershed moment in this multi-year investigation, the significance of this message bears pointing out. Captain Chotvacs wrote that the psychologist found me fit for full duty, Commander Borox had full knowledge of this investigation and yet believed in my capabilities to the point that he gave me an interim Top Secret clearance and permission to re-enlist in the Navy for six years. It was a matter of official record that my performance to date had been above par in every single job I been assigned. Captain Chotvacs had called Commander Borox and discussed this issue (ref b). Hard work? Yeah, it pays off. Yet, the most important part is the last two lines of Captain Chotvacs message; unless directed otherwise every effort will be made to retain me in the Navy and my interim Top Secret clearance will continue. This was a day to celebrate.

I didn't win the full battle. On July 30, 1991 the Central Adjudication Facility sent a message to Captain Chotvacs stating that I was authorized a Top Secret clearance but denied the Special Compartmented Information portion of my clearance. They denied the SCI portion based upon my completed background investigation which was signed as "finalized" on October 25, 1990. The closing sentence of their message to me stated: "However, you are cautioned that receipt of any derogatory information in the future will be cause for reconsideration of our decision."

A Top Secret clearance allowed me to stay in my current job and would also afford me the opportunity to continue to serve in the Submarine Force, but it limited several other career options. I couldn't become a Naval Officer and work in any type of specialized mission (Intelligence,

Cryptology, etc.) without the SCI portion of a security clearance, but I had a little over three more years of college to complete and realized that if I were to ever become a Naval Officer, I would have to face that hurdle when it presented itself to me. I still had one more battle to get through before I was cleared to serve in the Navy without reservation. The matter of my administrative separation had to be addressed, and Captain Chotvacs was preparing for battle.

On August 20, 1991 Submarine Group Five sent the following message to the Bureau of Naval Personnel, which would make the final determination if I would be administratively separated for fraudulent enlistment, or allowed to continue to serve:

From: Commander Submarine Group 5
To: Bureau of Naval Personnel (PERS 83)
Subj: QM2 (SS) PAUL B TRIPP, USN
Ref: (a) NAVMILPERSCOMINST 1910.1D
       (b) MILPERSMAN 3630300 AND 3610200
       (c) Phone conversation between COMSUBGRU FIVE Security Manager (LT Hellen) and USS CINCINNATI (SSN 693) Commanding Officer (Commander Borox)
Encl: (1) DON CAF ltr of 16 May 1991
       (2) COMSUBGRU FIVE ltr of 03 July 1991
       (3) DON CAF message on 30 July 1991
       (4) DON CAF letter of 06 August 1991
       (5) Various service record data

1. References (a) and (b) dictate that individuals who have experienced homosexual incidents prior to enlistment should be considered for administrative separation. During the conduct of a security investigation of subject member, two possible homosexual incidents which occurred prior to enlistment were revealed. These incidents are discussed in enclosure (1). The first incident occurred at age nine and was a non-consequential experience typical of childhood development. The second incident occurred in August 1986 and was the result of coercion and immature judgment caused by situational vulnerability as a result of subject member not being able to meet basic living expenses.

2. The incidents cited above and the questions of subject member's sexual orientation have been extensively investigated by this command, DON CAF, and subject's previous command, USS CINCINNATI (SSN 693). This process included a review by a clinical psychologist who found subject fit for full duty and that there was insufficient evidence to support that subject is homosexual. While several references developed during a security investigation speculated that subject might have a homosexual orientation, the speculations are not supported by fact nor do they cite any witnessed genuine homosexual acts by or with the subject. While a positive statement cannot be made as to subject's sexual preference, subject emphatically denies that he is homosexual, and there is no evidence other than speculation to suggest that the subject has a homosexual orientation.

3. This command, subject's previous command (USS CINCINNATI (SSN693)), DON CAF and the clinical psychologist as discussed in reference (c) and enclosures (2) through (4), all agree that there is no behavioral, mental or emotional condition, or illness which could cause a defect in judgment or reliability, nor does the subject's history preclude his ability to serve with distinction in the Navy and to fully safeguard classified material. Reference (c) re-enforces the foregoing in that USS CINCINNATI, having full knowledge of the Defense Investigative Report (enclosure (1)) favorably adjudicated subject's security clearance, continued his participation in the Personnel Reliability Program (PRP) and reenlisted him in December 1990. Subsequently, this command and DON CAF with full knowledge of the subject's background favorably adjudicated a TOP SECRET security clearance for subject member (enclosures 2 through 4)).

4. This command is resolute in its opinion that subject member should not be administratively separated for the two pre-service isolated incidents cited above. Subject's service record is spotless, in fact commendatory as evidenced by the documentation provided as enclosure (5). Our strong endorsement for his retention is indicated by our recommendation that he also be retained in the Submarine Force.

5. Formal processing for administrative separation has not been completed, and unless otherwise directed, will not be initiated.

In this particular case, formal processing should not be necessary as it is believed that the documentation provided fully supports subject's continued service. It is requested, however, that the appropriate record action be taken to indicate Navy's finding for retention.

6. My point of contact regarding this issue is LT Hellen. Signed – C.J. CHOTVACS, Chief of Staff

A Navy Command can fight for a sailor if it believes that the sailor is worth keeping, but when a serious offense occurs the matter is oftentimes left up to the Bureau of Naval Personnel. There is no doubt that Captain Chotvacs' letter had significant weight in the final decision, but ultimately, the decision was not up to anyone but the Bureau of Naval Personnel.

While I knew that I could be kicked out of the Navy, the reinstatement of my security clearance had given me a sense of hope, a belief that I would indeed be retained. I had no more conversation left in me, I was all talked out. I had been talking about this issue for three years, an issue that followed me from Quartermaster "A" school, to Submarine School to the USS CINCINNATI SSN-693 and now to Submarine Group Five. Florida to Connecticut to Virginia to California. The time, effort, manpower and money that had been spent on investigating the claim that some people thought I was a homosexual were staggering. They had not found any solid proof –- none, and yet, the investigators continued to pull up rock after rock, and repeatedly deny my clearance.

On September 13, 1991 the final answer arrived in a message from the Bureau of Personnel:

BUPERS (DTG 131938ZSEP91), the subject line of this message stated "Retain and warn QM2 Paul B. Tripp." The remarks were as follows:

1. The following Page 13 entry is to be made in the member's service record: You are being retained in the Naval Service, in spite of the Defense Investigative Service Special Background Investigative report of 16 November 1988. Action appropriate as the situation was

a departure from your usual and customary behavior, the situation is unlikely to recur, your continued presence in the Navy is consistent with proper discipline, good order and morale and your Commanding Officer's desires. However, any further deficiencies in performance and/or conduct may result in processing for administrative separation. Such processing will consider all deficiencies and/or misconduct during your current enlistment, both prior to and subsequent to the date of this action, and may result in a discharge under other than honorable conditions. This authority for retention does not waive requirements for selected assignment policies.

With the final piece of correspondence written, the Bureau of Personnel made a determination that I would be retained in the Navy. I had managed to stand my ground, plead my case, engender the support of those around me and withstand the continued investigation along with the heavy weight of a possible administrative separation.

Not content with the final answer on my security clearance, Captain Chotvacs called me into his office on September 26, 1991 and told me that he wanted to try again and write an appeal to the Naval Intelligence Command asking that I be granted SCI eligibility. I didn't realize the full impact of this denial, but Captain Chotvacs knew of my desire to become a Naval Officer and it was his goal to ensure that I was afforded every future opportunity to succeed. To that end, I wrote the following statement and submitted it to Captain Chotvacs for him to send on to the Naval Intelligence Command:

27 September 1991 – a statement from Paul Tripp to the Naval Intelligence Command:

1. I was raised in a broken family, torn between my mother and my father, the latter being a manic dysfunctional alcoholic. I have never had a strong male role model to mold myself after, and because of this I have been labeled emotionally sensitive by my peers. While the two incidents of my youth are embarrassing, the first one being of molestation at age nine, and the second being manipulation in a very vulnerable situation, these incidents are not such that I would act in any disloyal fashion against the security of

the United States. I am not homosexual and I am not subject to blackmail or coercion.

2. I would like to continue my career in the United States Navy. The special operations typical to submarines require that I be able to access SCI information to advance and function as a senior member of the submarine force. I request reconsideration and adjudication of my case so that SCI access is possible. I am available for any follow on interviews that are necessary.

The Navy sent the following message, with my statement included, to the Naval Intelligence Command in early October 1991:

From: Commander Submarine Group 5
To: Commander Naval Intelligence Command
Subject: APPEAL OF SENSITIVE COMPARTMENTED INFOR-MATION (SCI) ACCESS

1. Forwarded strongly recommending approval of Petty Officer Tripp's appeal to his SCI ineligibility.

2. Petty Officer Tripp has consistently done an outstanding job in all assignments since reporting to COMSUBGRU FIVE Staff. He is a highly motivated sailor who has shown absolutely no indication of poor judgment, unreliability, or compromise of integrity of classified information in any situation. I am totally confident that he has the loyalty, presence of mind and foresight to perform any job requiring access to classified material without risk of compromise. I believe the information contained in his investigation is unsubstantiated and this issue is now a matter of record.

Signed, C.J. CHOTVACS, Chief of Staff

Several weeks later the Naval Intelligence Command responded to Submarine Group Five and denied my eligibility for an SCI clearance once again. There was no other avenue in which an appeal could be submitted. I had been denied an SCI clearance for the second time and the matter was now considered closed. While I still held a Top Secret clearance, the SCI denial would come back to haunt me one last time. A time when I least expected it.

PART TWO

1 CORINTHIANS 10:13

(Age 24)

I first started taking aerobics in Montana, but San Diego is where I started teaching it. Exercise brought me unlimited joy and a feeling of security with my flat stomach disappearing into my spandex shorts without so much as a hint of a muffin top. I prided myself on being in shape, running close to ten miles every day at lunch while I routed submarines in and out of the California sunshine. I used exercise as the cup that quenched all of my thirsts: sexual, work stress, anxiety about my life, my conflict with God. It was my answer to everything.

Perched on the stage at one of the premiere gyms in San Diego, I shouted out commands to packed roomfuls of people while the dance music blared overhead. I was particular about my aerobics music as I wanted to be as motivated by music as my students, so I had a local DJ make each cassette tape tailored for my classes. Fun, carefree and a ninety-minute workout, I had developed a loyal following of fitness fanatics and was always looking forward to spinning around on the stage.

My most loyal follower was a woman named Katy Medora. Standing a robust 5'2" in height, with black hair, as petite as a blade of grass and a zest for exercise that rivaled Richard Simmons, Katy was my biggest fan. She also had a love for Christ that I was unaware of until her definition of Jesus bumped into mine one day in the gym parking lot. Unbeknownst to me, Katy had been praying for me as I called out the cues of my step aerobics classes. A love of fitness and a love for Christ, Katy became my best friend and as you will find out, my savior here on earth.

Too scared to admit that I was in the military, I told Katy that I worked at AT&T. Pardon me if I was short on pride for wearing the cloth of our nation. I had just been through a several-year investigation in which the Defense Investigative Service investigators had tried to expose my life to anyone who would listen, and get me kicked out of the military in the process. As far as anyone in San Diego was concerned, I worked in the tallest building in downtown San Diego. I didn't have any close friends in San Diego at this point, so the details of my job felt more like an omission of truth to protect myself than an outright lie. At least that's what I told myself until Katy told me one day after class that she had gone downtown to the AT&T building to bring me lunch, and they told her that they had never heard of me. Caught in yet another untoward circumstance due to the military rules and regulations of making it illegal for homosexuals to serve, I took Katy to lunch and served her a big plate of honesty.

I fell in love with Katy Medora in the same way that I believe Christ falls in love with his children. Unconditional, deep, and with more affection and love than I can express in words. She became a confidant, a best friend, a mother, a girlfriend and the only person on earth whom I grew to trust with my entire being. As time slipped by I slipped Katy more and more of my life story, coming clean on every sordid detail about my past. With her soft brown eyes looking into mine, she listened with the heart of Christ and the understanding of Job. Katy would end most of our meetings in a request for prayer, where we would bow our heads and thank Christ for our friendship. Christ, you truly did deliver an angel to me here on earth.

As my friendship with Katy blossomed, so did my involvement with the Medora family. I spent countless hours in their home in fellowship, taking walks on the beach and discussing my life's situation, including my sexual preference. Katy and her husband Jeremy guided me biblically, but without the fire and brimstone of Pastor Valentine, and I slowly became curious about God's plan for my life. If you take a moment and think about that concept for your own life, what does that mean to you? For me, I had been through a rough childhood, experienced life abroad, lived through adventures in Hawaii and Los Angeles and was now serving our country in the US Navy. I began to question the purpose of my existence. Why was I here on earth? I became hungry to understand how I could contribute to a cause larger than myself that would have a positive impact beyond what I dreamed possible.

Hungry for His word, my hunger for an interpersonal relationship with another man continued to grow at an equal pace. I knew I was gay and had come to the point in my life where I could openly admit this fact to the Medora family, but I still hadn't learned how to reconcile my sexual desires with a gay lifestyle. They seemed like two pieces of a puzzle that didn't belong together, and when I added my understanding of God's will into the mix, I became even more confused as to how I would be able to put these pieces together to create a masterpiece.

The Navy during the day, college at night, aerobics classes, fellowship with the Medora family on the weekends and gay bars at night, my life was compartmentalized neater than a shoe rack at Nordstrom. Every single time I tried to introduce one aspect of my life to another, chaos broke out and the possibility of exposing my private life to military authorities loomed closer. I didn't have the heart to disappoint Captain Chotvacs, and yet my perpetual unsatisfied hard-on kept me mentally distracted and on edge for the majority of the time. Exercise, exercise, exercise was the only way I was able to keep the wolves at bay so I could focus on my work, schooling and the word of God.

As I came to understand the word of God in a new way, I had a re-alization that all I had ever wanted in my life was to be accepted. I had always wanted to be able to walk into a locker room and be slapped on the ass like one of the guys, and think nothing of it. I was sure I could belch and fart with the best of them. I longed to be able to pick up a gun and shoot some deer with just enough stubble on my face to make me a real warrior. I never intended to define my life through the notes of musical theater or the isolation of being an exchange student, but what else did I have? When I joined the theater troupe of "Fiddler on The Roof" and began fooling around with the lead, it felt so natural. It was as easy as walking into my first gay party at age seventeen. I felt at home, a place where acceptance ruled supreme. Until this point, being amongst gay men was the only place I felt freedom, without conflict and truly authen-tic to myself.

As I struggled for how I would come to understand acceptance in my life, my nightlife at the gay bars in San Diego became a source of conflict for me. I attempted to seek out men who had a heart for Christ, who wanted to discuss what they believed to be their life's calling – but I was always left with the calling card of a phone number or the invitation for a one night stand. Try as I might, I left the bars with a dance beat in my head and an open palm of loneliness. The only open arms I knew I could walk into were those of the Medoras, and Jesus Christ himself.

BUD

(Age 24)

Meeting him was an accident. I had just finished a three hour marathon on the dance floor of Rich's, one of the hottest gay clubs in San Diego, when I headed into the bathroom to take a piss and wipe my brow dry one last time. Disinterested in everything but the main man of the C&C Music Factory or Madonna, I avoided eye contact with almost everyone that night –- everyone except Bud.

As I pushed open the door to leave, I pushed it right into Bud's face. Apologetic and feeling a bit embarrassed by my military march out of the gay bar, I stopped to make sure he was OK. Buzzed haircut, sharp strong features, a chest as round and firm as Bunker Hill with piercing blue eyes to match, Bud told me that the only way I would be forgiven was if I would grab a drink with him down the street. Another man, another drink, another night, another opportunity for meaningless convenient sex, I did my best to back away from his invitation, but he batted away all my excuses. Where was I going at 1 a.m.? Straight to the bar down the street with Bud.

Bud was as cocky as my Aunt Glenda's rooster and had the brawn to back it up. Flirtatious but coy, he entertained my whimsy of asking his purpose here on earth and if he believed in God. One hour turned to two hours which ended at 5 a.m. in a puddle of used words and philosophical meanderings. In the four hours since we met I had learned that Bud loved the Lord, was conflicted about how to lead an authentic "openly" gay life, was a Marine Corps Officer and believed he also had a higher calling in his life. Military, God and a purpose beyond himself, Bud was the first man I felt like I had made a real connection with, a connection that didn't start or end in the bedroom and a connection that was not borne out of desperation or need.

I told Bud I worked at AT&T as the comingling of lives between a military officer and an enlisted man is forbidden outside of the workplace. Unwilling to sacrifice my newfound relationship, I avoided all talk of work while Bud told me he was in town for a long weekend, getting ready to move overseas. Friday night, Saturday, Saturday night, Sunday and Sunday night found us traversing the city engaged in the type of esoteric conversation that fed my soul. Spending time with Bud encouraged me to pursue my dream of becoming a Naval Officer, as he was one of the few I had met who were also gay. If it's possible to fall in love with the ideal of what a person represents, then I was head over heels in love with Bud.

Educated, masculine, career minded, with a love for Christ that he still hadn't figured out, I drew scenario after scenario in my head of how he and I might have a life together someday. I gave him my favorite book, "The Education of Little Tree," while he gave me the hope that gay men like me did in fact exist. On our last night together I helped him pack his things.

His trunk packed an unexpected punch — a picture of a woman and three children — which he never mentioned during our past four days together. As he came out of the bathroom I confronted him, and he confessed his truth. Like Anne Frank he had kept his wife and three children hidden away, ensconced beneath his jockey underwear that I knew all too well. With no mention of a family, I felt as if I had just spent the last four days with a traitor.

This newfound truth was a baseball-bat blow to my head. I had never met a man like Bud, I had never met a man who shared the same spiritual conflict, I had never met a man who had same-sex desires who also had no desire to lead an openly gay life, and . . . it looked like I still hadn't. I had fallen for Bud's sincerity hook, line and sinker, and the discovery of a wife and kids had suddenly called every word into question. I couldn't seem to wrap my head around how a person could be so deceitful in the face of such honesty. We had shared so much, and I had felt a sense of hope that I would be able to meet another man who shared my same life's struggle. To be faced with the truth that the last four days of our lives together had been a lie, kicked the nonsense of all future hope right out of me.

I couldn't listen to him as he sat on the bed and redefined himself. Four days into what I believed was a genuine exchange between two people, I neither had the desire nor the heart to watch him shake the Etch-a-Sketch of his life and redraw it again. I listened to him for about fifteen minutes and then walked out the door, with a lump in my throat. Not knowing what else to do, I got into my car, prayed and recalled my favorite verse, 1 Corinthians 10:13: No temptation has overtaken you except what is common to mankind. God is faithful; he will not let you be tempted beyond what you can bear. But when you are tempted, he will also provide a way out so that you can endure it.

Not wanting to see him again, yet unable to stay away, I picked Bud up the next morning and drove him to the airport. A holiday Monday, the roads were wide open and desolate. I longed for a traffic jam so I could probe his heart, but it was clear to me that God had a different plan. Bud had been exposed to me for a reason, and my passenger was the most beautiful liar I had ever met. As I dropped him off he looked at the ground sheepishly, apologizing, and we shook hands. I wanted to hug him and I also wanted to beat the shit out of him. Unsure when or if I would see him again or how I would reconcile the past four days in my mind, I got into my car and drove away.

Scheduled to teach an early morning holiday aerobics class, I drove through tears to the Body Workshop. I slowly felt myself asphyxiating at the realization that the homosexual lifestyle might not ever bring me the happiness I desired. The tape in my mind was on constant playback and my hands were busy flicking ashes out the car window as I rewound the Whitney Houston songs playing on my car radio. Bud was a fake; Bud was a fake, a complete fake. Between Whitney's voice and my own internal shrieks, I couldn't help but think that there was no hope of peace for my homosexual self.

Blinded by tears, my alter ego began searching for a gun as I drove my car looking for a semblance of truth. Somewhere between the San Diego airport and the Body Workshop in La Jolla I cemented the thought that I would never have a world that consisted of love and gay relationships. Bud had shown me that I either had to commit to an openly gay lifestyle — which I did not want — or go to the dark side with a pistol in my hand. His example was clear; there was no in between unless I wanted to live a life of lies with a hidden wife and children stored away in a trunk. The choice between men and love had never been boiled down so barren before my eyes, and I now felt paralyzed in its clutches. It was as if the blinders on my eyes had been removed from Christ Himself, as Bud showed me a torment so great I had to shield my soul from the ugliness of its' truth. It hurt, oh God, it hurt.

When I pulled into the parking lot I jumped out of my car as if it were on fire. I didn't care who was watching or what anyone else was thinking. I needed a phone; I needed to call my stepmother, Lynn. What a savior she had been in my life so many times before. Although our relationship was strained due to her marital problems with my father, I had no one else.

I couldn't call the Medora family for I had been working so hard to put Christ before my sexual desires that Bud's betrayal felt too big to verbalize. Lynn, the woman who wrote notes and stuffed them in my sixth grade lunch bag would have the answer — she always did. I picked up the payphone and dialed, whimpering like a hurt animal. I got a busy signal. In that moment, I believed that the meter on my life had expired.

Unsure where to turn, I got back into my car and concocted a plan to end my life. Inconsolable, I put the car in reverse, paralleling my life's story. As I backed up, a familiar gold Audi pulled into the parking lot. Katy? Katy? She had arrived at the studio close to forty-five minutes ahead of schedule, which was atypical for her. With a tap on my window, I pulled the car back into its parking spot and turned off the engine.

Katy got into the car and as she opened the door it was as if the breath of Christ himself had entered. I leaned over and put my head into her lap and sobbed. She sat there and held me, not asking one single question. As I lay there with my head in her lap I felt a struggle for my soul that made it difficult to breath. I could feel the opposite ends of my spirit being pulled in two different directions.

Un-reconciled between my personal and professional life, I lay in Katy's lap exhausted from the conflict I had been dealing with for so many years. I felt a grumbling in my soul to give up my earthly struggle and give my life completely back to Christ. My tears were for the decision I believed I had to make, for the errors of my past and for the love I had always wanted, but that eluded me. After a half an hour of tears and torment, I grabbed Katy's hand and asked the Lord to help me walk away from the homosexual lifestyle. I begged Him to deliver me from my same-sex sexual desires. I promised Him that I would follow Him to the ends of the earth, if He would promise to deliver me and bring me a wife who could love me unconditionally and accept my past.

The next day I changed my phone number, packed up my car, moved into a hotel until I could find a new place to live, changed my email, and deleted every single gay friend out of my personal contacts. I was dead serious about ending this struggle in my life, and while I could have accomplished this through suicide, I believed that God had yet to show me the reason for living. My decision to turn my life back over to God didn't feel like a choice, it felt like my only option.

I made good on my promise, and so did God.

REPARATIVE THERAPY
(Age 25)

With my legs as wobbly as a newborn calf, Katy became the walk-ing stick that helped me move through life. She had heard of a program called NARTH — The National Association of Reparative Therapy for Homosexuals — headed by Dr. Nicolosi, and got me the information I requested. Within a few weeks we found a counselor together, I found a twelve step program at a local church and I ordered every single book I could on reparative therapy and same-sex attraction. Every night after work, I read copious amounts of information on reparative therapy. There were many men who had "claimed" victory in Christ and were now lead-ing what they believed to be a successful heterosexual lifestyle. Within weeks I was sharing in a group setting, talking to my counselor twice a week and in continued fellowship with the Medora family.

If I wasn't talking I was praying, and I believed with my entire heart and soul that my obedience to Christ would manifest itself with dimin-ished sexual desire and quite possibly a wife. I realize that some of you may think I was delusional, others may think I was crazy and yet some of you may believe that I was a young man who had defied the will of God and was now paying a price for my sins. For those of you who have never experienced the call of God's will on your life, I can understand your judg-ment. The majority of us have no ear for anything but ourselves. I was that young man, choking on the silence of my sexuality to the point that it caused several traumatic events to unfold. I was neither true to God, nor was I true to myself. My military uniform forced me into a closet of inauthenticity that crippled my ability to do my job, kept me in a state of fear over being turned in, and paralyzed my ability to think clearly and be honest with the investigators. I was unable to have an authentic gay rela-tionship due to my spiritual conflict with God and the fact that a potential boyfriend could have ruined my career by outing me. I was also unable to be fully accepted as a Christian leading an active gay lifestyle, and had been told so starting with Pastor Valentine.

I believed that to be brought into the true calling of Christ was to have my life profoundly altered. It had happened to me the summer of my eighth grade year when the Holy Spirit poured from my mouth in the form of speaking in tongues, and I also believed Christ reached out and touched my heart through my chance encounter with Bud. I wasn't confused about the fact that Christ wanted a foothold in my life, and as I moved through reparative therapy I became convinced that Bud was the vehicle Christ chose to get my attention. Reparative therapy didn't claim that homosexuality is a biblical sin, at least not during my participation or time with my counselor. Instead, this program allowed me to evaluate the external influences that might have contributed to my same-sex attraction. Was I convinced that I was born gay? Yes I was. Was I convinced that God could deliver me from same-sex attraction if I disavowed the lifestyle and lived a life according to His will? Yes I was.

At the age of twenty-four I began unpacking my backpack of homo-sexuality and took an inventory of everything inside. I became aware of the fact that what I found exotic as a child was the masculinity of men, which is the same thing I found exotic as an adult. I read about how ho-mosexual men tend to sexualize encounters with other men due to child-hood deficits of not being accepted. I tore apart the incidents of bullying, being beat up, not accepted in school, my parental examples and continued sense of needing to guard myself against everything and everyone, relying solely on my own strength to power through life. Week after week and chapter after chapter I worked through the process of trying to understand my same-sex attraction from a viewpoint I had never seen. If reality was the necessary viewpoint from which I had understood my homosexuality and the illusions and distortions of my life, it was God to whom I prayed to show me unseen landscapes.

I was feverish with the hope that I could have a breakthrough in my life and be free from the burden of my homosexuality. While physically pleasurable, it had stained so many aspects of my personal and professional life that the price of living this life was something I could no longer afford. The Clark Fork Christian Center had taught me that while homosexual-ity is a sin, there is a marked difference between homosexual identity and homosexual acts. Pastor Valentine used to tell me that he understood I identified myself as homosexual, but to act on it was an abomination of God. I took what he said to heart. For as long as I could remember I had walked through the world in full battle gear trying to deny myself the pleasure of sexual acts, losing every battle I had fought.

Now, with the wind of God at my back and the hope of all hope in my heart, I believed that change was possible. While I didn't deny my homosexual nature, I made a concerted effort to cease all homosexual acts and thoughts while I made my way through my personal inventory. Success came in spurts, like carbonated soda spraying out of a bottle. While I did manage to stop all physical encounters with men, self-pleasure continued to be the one dragon I couldn't manage to slay. I worked to gain control of my thoughts through prayer and fasting.

It took several months for me to feel as if I had made any real progress. Work, college at night, reparative group therapy, reparative counseling, and fellowship with the Medora family helped my mind absorb new concepts while sprouting out tiny new blades of understanding. My trepidation had turned to joy and was working its way towards grief as I mourned the loss of the circle of gay friends I had worked so hard to develop. Shut out of my life like a slammed door, I was forced to acknowledge that I would never see them again. No more music, no more dancing at Rich's gay bar, and no more exciting meetings with men like Bud, the reality of reparative therapy hit me quite hard.

I was never told that I had to change my sexual orientation by the NARTH organization. Instead, I was encouraged to look within in an attempt to understand my same-sex feelings. Having stuffed them away in the closets of Montana and the military, my reparative therapy counselor's office was a safe haven where I could speak openly about my deepest fears and darkest fantasies. Sharing my past illuminated my homosexual feelings, normalized them really, while I consciously chose to walk my life down a heterosexual path — a path that I had learned from the Church, and society, was normal. Everything I had come to understand about myself was up for discussion and change, and change is exactly what I did.

JUDY

(Age 25)

Black and white checkered shorts with a red shirt; I couldn't tell if she was a victory or cautionary flag in my race of life. Long brown hair, clean cut fingernails, brown shoes and a brown purse - she chatted non-stop about everything imaginable while perched precariously on top of a bar stool at one of the local dives in Pacific Beach. That – was our first date.

I met Judy in my aerobics class. A student with more left feet than right, her cousin Kris introduced us before I could change out of my sweat-soaked clothes, and within the first few minutes Judy invited me on a bike ride. Wind, blowing sand, crowded beaches and dirt, going for a bike ride sounded like as much fun as getting my teeth cleaned. I bowed out of the pedaling adventure but we exchanged numbers, and the day after my twenty-fifth birthday, still nursing a hangover from a drunken night at home trying to make sense of my new life, we went out for a beer.

This was my first real date with a woman. While I had experienced a couple of sexual encounters with women prior to this night, this was the first time I had ever allowed myself to date a woman, which of course had the possible outcome of marriage. I was scared shitless. All kinds of thoughts were crashing together in my brain. What woman would take a gay man as her husband? How would I explain my past to the people I had yet to meet? Like a recovering alcoholic, would I always be "doubted" if I proclaimed I was reformed through reparative therapy? What would I do when I felt a sexual urge for a man?

Over the past several months, some of my old gay friends tried to track me down to see if I was OK, but I never responded to their re-quests. How was I supposed to tell them that I had just experienced a spiritual transition that transported me to an entirely different plane? I didn't feel like the same person that they knew, and I knew I didn't want the conflict of living a gay lifestyle anymore, but how was I supposed to verbalize that? How do you explain the feeling of the Holy Spirit running through your body as tears pour out of your eyes? How do you describe the moment when you know that God has spoken in your ear with a loving kiss of reassurance that everything will be OK? How was I supposed to verbalize to my friends that Jesus had chosen me to come and walk with him again? There are no words to speak aloud to those who do not understand, and so I remained silent with my past while putting my future in God's hands.

As I readied myself for my date, I choked out a mournful prayer in English and in tongues telling God that I had honored His word by walking away from homosexuality and was trusting in Him to give me the strength to see this night through. He did.

Date #2. Judy was waiting for me on our second date as I pulled up to the church of Horizon Christian Fellowship. This church had become the ointment that I spread all over my body and soul on the weekends to keep me from temptation and quench my thirst for spiritual feeding throughout the week. I had invited Judy to join me, wanting her to see every single side of me before we got too far along. Raised in Oregon, Judy family wasn't the church going type. I'm not sure Judy had ever been to a church like this one; charismatic, music filled, hands waving and speaking in tongues —- she was in for a real surprise.

Pastor Mike MacIntosh took center stage once the music died down and we bowed our heads to pray. I wish I could remember his message that night, but it's now part of my forgotten history. What I do remember is that when the "altar call" came forward for those to accept Jesus Christ as their Lord and Savior, Judy raised her hand. I didn't realize she felt the calling of Christ until she stood up and walked towards the front of the stage, openly acknowledging that she was ready to love God as much as He was ready to show her His forgiveness and love. I had prayed, she had come to church, and she had accepted Christ as her Lord and Savior.

Standing in the front of the church, Judy was handed a Bible and a few phone numbers to call should she have any questions about her new walk with God. Flabbergasted, I had a few questions I wanted to ask but it didn't seem like an appropriate time to blurt them out since Judy had no idea that I was a homosexual working through reparative therapy. Together we walked out of the church and stood in the parking lot for several hours talking about what had just happened in her life. She had no intention of giving her life to Christ when she walked into the church that night, but God clearly had a different plan in mind.

As I lay in bed that night, I openly acknowledged God's calling on Judy's life as a sign from Him to me. I wasn't sure how I was going to spill the beans about my past, but I knew that I had to tell her before too much time had passed between us. There's something magical that happens in your life when you accept Christ, and I knew her heart was tender and open. Formulating the words in my head, I sought strength, through prayer, to deliver my news and fill in the blanks of my past. Judy deserved honesty no matter what path our relationship took. Her journey and mine had officially begun.

THIRD DATE

(Age 25)

Since our first date Judy and I talked every single night on the phone for several hours. I loved Judy's laugh, it was infectious, and so we talked and laughed until my eyes got too heavy to keep open. Bedtime, even way back then, was always earlier than most. 9 p.m. was the perfect moment to crawl into a fetal position and let my world disappear. Consistent with my childhood, I was an early riser, getting up at 5 a.m. to start my day. There's something so magical and unpretentious about the morning. It's a space of time where you can look out upon the world and watch it come awake. No hustle, no bustle — just the silence of a sunrise and the quiet voice of God.

I had experienced so many inauthentic relationships due to my own inabilities to get honest; I knew that I had to tell Judy the truth about my past. I played it over and over in my head, and each time I said the phrase, "I am gay" it sounded as abrupt as stating I had killed someone.

The sun had set and we had just returned from having dinner. Pulling back in front of my apartment complex on Georgia Street, I knew this would be a defining moment in our relationship. Too scared to go it alone, I grasped her hands and we prayed together — a standard prayer that didn't allude to my past. Complete with our thanks to Jesus, I told her I needed to tell her the truth about a situation in my life.

No fanfare and no drumrolls, I laid my homosexuality out on the table in full view for her to see. I told her about the military investigations, my struggle with sexuality and the fact that the only other people in my life who knew about the transition I had undertaken were the Medora family. I gave it to her 100% straight — no mixed messages, no hidden meanings, no half-truths. I was a gay man who had turned his life over to Christ and was now undergoing reparative therapy with a counselor and relying on the spiritual assistance of the Medoras. I laid it out as black and white as the checkered shorts she wore on our first date.

We sat there in silence holding hands, and she asked if we could pray. She didn't pass judgment, she didn't explode in disbelief, and in fact she didn't say much of anything. She listened, we prayed and she got out of my car and made her way towards her vehicle. I had no idea what she was thinking nor did I ask. I allowed my truth to sit between us in silence, giving her the moment to evaluate this new reality. Standing at her car, she reached out and gave me a big hug and thanked me for my honesty. With that, she drove away.

I suppose a bit of narrative is apropos at this stage of my story, for some of you may be wondering if I was a bisexual trapped in the body of a homosexual male. My truth is that I was gay, believed I was born gay and while I had experienced minimal sexual contact with women, I identified as a homosexual –- one hundred percent gay. In the same way that I never knew God until the eighth grade, I had never known any sexual feelings other than those towards men. All of my sexual fantasies involved men, never women, and while a revved up sex drive could have allowed me to "perform" to a picture of a naked woman for the military investigators, that's only because I was in my early twenties. I chose to enter reparative therapy in an attempt to reconcile my life according to the word of God, military standards and societal norms. Changing the object of my sexual desire was as foreign to me as it would be to you. With that cleared up, let's get back to what happened next.

My admissions to Judy felt like I had put a detour sign on the road of our relationship and yet I felt like I had also opened up a part of myself. I had become truly authentic with another individual for the second time in my life. I called the Medora family and told them the news. While surprised that I had shared so much, they had also come to understand that I wasn't a man who could hold back when something personal needed to be said. Investigations aside, I believed in telling the truth and giving other people the facts as directly as possible. Judy had the facts.

I didn't hear from her the next day, but the day after that she called me and asked me out for coffee, which led us to our fifth, sixth and seventh dates. With my admission clear between us, it was clear that we were now officially dating. I'm not sure if we ever proclaimed this between us, but as I introduced her to the Medora family and she introduced me to her group of friends, we fell into the familiar framework of a couple. As Christians, we laid out the ground rules of intimacy, which meant no sex until marriage, and although we hadn't broached the subject, after several months I felt the stirrings of an emotional connection that I believed could lead us down the aisle.

As slowly as a flower blooming in the spring, our lives became inter-twined. The Medora family welcomed her into their home where we spent many, many, many days in fellowship together. As you know, Katy was the impetus that changed my heart back to God and my biggest supporter in my walk with Christ. Jeremy was the cornerstone of our Bible studies and a man with whom I could discuss the struggles of my sexuality. Both of them were fully aware of my transition as the four of us discussed every single aspect of what it meant to walk with Christ through the billowing storm of life. The windows of our collective honesty were flung wide open and we talked about everything from salvation to masturbation.

Judy's friends resided at the opposite end of our honesty spectrum. Her roommate Lynn had no idea of my past, nor did Debbie, Mike, Chuck, Darcy, Wendy, Ken or the numerous other people in Judy's life. I left the decision up to Judy if she wanted to share my circumstances with them but it was her choice, always her choice, to remain silent on this issue. Since Judy didn't want to share my story with any of her friends, there was a barrier between the intimacy I wanted and the one that I was able to have.

As our relationship grew, I found myself growing restless with how my new life forced me to be inauthentic in a new way. I wanted to shout my newfound freedom from the homosexual lifestyle from every roof top in San Diego but I had to keep silent at work, silent amongst Judy's friends and silent to every single person who wasn't in a personal relation-ship with God. Even those who walked hand-in-hand with Christ had a hard time grasping my personal transition. There's a flash of horror that moves across a person's eyes when you tell them something that is beyond their comprehension. Admitting that I had walked away from an active homosexual lifestyle to follow Christ always caused an electric reaction, if only for the briefest of seconds. Over time, Judy and I understood that not everyone would be able to accept our situation and so our closest friends became the Medora family to include Jeremy and Katy's son Mike and his wife Colleen.

Born again and actively working a reparative therapy program, my sexual desires no longer dictated my personal behavior. I still sexualized most of my encounters with men and masturbated to the same old fantasies, but over time each one of these acts diminished to the point that I could become curious about the person, instead of their penis. Judy used to joke that it was the first time in her life she was with a man who wasn't checking out women in her presence. I was checking them out, but it was usually to see if their shoes matched their purses, what their accessories looked like and what kind of hairstyle they were sporting. Judy never had to worry about me cheating with a woman –- that much we both knew for sure.

My transition into a heterosexual relationship was accompanied by gusts of angry winds and withering emotions. On most days I felt like a tree shedding its leaves, preparing itself for the winter. I was in the throes of making my old self die while trying to reinvent myself and find happiness within a new lifestyle. As newfound Christians, Judy and I agreed that sex before marriage would not glorify the sacrifices we had made together, and our goal was to glorify and honor the Lord. I was able to get to know Judy, spend time with Judy and grow in my own sexual understanding of myself without the pressure of sex. Admittedly it was a convenient choice for me, but in that space of time I also believed that if I could deny myself any sexual pleasure I would be rewarded by God on the day we consummated our marriage.

Judy had agreed that she would walk with me through the reparative therapy process and I appreciated her willingness, but it was a promise she couldn't fulfill. Judy had no understanding of the gay lifestyle, didn't have one gay friend growing up and through no fault of her own there wasn't a crash course in the nuance of emotions that surround walking away from the only part of a life that has ever brought pleasure. The only place I felt safe to open up and share was when we were with the Medora family, and rarely did Judy and I talk about my transition when we were alone. I had attempted to bring it up with her on several occasions, but the conversation typically fell flat between us, sucking the air out of the moment, so I learned to stay silent on my struggle when it was just the two of us.

It was the one of the darkest times of my life and yet it was also one of the most authentic moments I have experienced. I opened myself up completely to what I believed to be the will of God, my counselor's guidance, the men of my twelve step program, the heart of my Church, the love of the Medora family and the acceptance of Judy.

ENGAGEMENT

(Age 25)

Four months after meeting Judy, we were engaged. I had been "out" of the gay lifestyle for about nine months when I asked her to marry me. She and I spent almost every night and weekend together praying, attending church and spending time with the Medora family. Four months felt more like two years, and we collectively believed that the Lord had somehow knitted our hearts together. I suppose you're wondering if I loved her and how in the world did I think a marriage was going to last after only knowing her for a few months – right?

When you turn your entire life over to Christ – I mean every single aspect to him – your life really does change in unexpected ways. I felt alive and awake for the first time in years; I was able to breathe without fear. I got my first taste of societal acceptance. I could hold Judy's hand walking down the street, without judgment. I could kiss her with a full display of public affection, and nobody took notice. When we went out I didn't have to worry about walking two steps ahead of her or wondering if we were going to run into anyone from work, for it didn't matter. I was able to socialize in society as one part of a fully integrated couple. I felt like I had walked into a world I had no idea even existed. My joy overwhelmed my doubts and I reveled in my new life. The engagement felt like a logical step in a series of events. I had no ruler from which to measure my past actions, so to me, a four month engagement felt completely natural.

Did I love her? Yes, I loved her. I loved the way she was patient and kind. I loved her heart for those less fortunate than she. I loved the way she could look at me and tell me I was being irrational without making me feel defensive. I loved the way she embraced the Lord and did not seem to judge my past. She stood by me as I made my way through my own personal journey, and I truly appreciated and loved her for that as well. Judy had a way of making everyone around her feel at ease, laugh with her and enjoy the moment. Yes, I loved her.

Like every couple, we had moments of tension and the more I relinquished control over my sexual identity, the more I felt I needed to control most of the other aspects in my life. I was probably more unwavering than needed, more opinionated than warranted and more outspoken than necessary. True to form, I was quick to verbalize my emotions and didn't typically take into consideration how my words affected other people until after I had spoken them. I was as immature as a two-year-old in this newly formed heterosexual relationship, and I have no doubt I spoke my truth loud and proud. I had hit my proverbial "bottom" in the parking lot of Body Workshop and as I made my way back into a new life I really didn't believe I had anything else to lose so I spoke my mind without restraint.

If I have regrets from those early days it is that I didn't propose to Judy when she and I were alone. There we were, at Pizzeria Uno, having dinner with Katy Medora after one of my aerobics classes. We had ordered salads and pizza and I had asked the waiter to put her engagement ring into her salad. As the three of us sat there talking and eating, Judy suddenly chomped on the ring, pulled it out of her mouth and it was then, I asked her to marry me. It's not a moment I look back on with joy. My truth is that I didn't have the courage to ask her alone, in an intimate moment where we could look into each other's eyes and feel the connection. I hadn't developed enough through my reparative therapy to be able to embrace that type of intimate connection with a woman, and so I chose a place and time that didn't serve to honor her. It should have been my first indication that I might not have been emotionally ready to get married, but at the time, I didn't see life that way. The three of us celebrated together –- the joy of the moment overpowering the awkwardness of what I was feeling inside. As always, we ended our meal in prayer.

The struggle of my same-sex attraction, while diminished, remained with me throughout my engagement to Judy. Some people become anorexic or bulimic to gain control, but as the wedding date grew closer I became more manic. There I was washing the windows on my car before it could leave the driveway, vacuuming Judy's hair out of the passenger's seat like a man possessed, and exercising as if I were preparing for the Ironman.

Judy had no sense of direction and used to get lost every time she drove to my house which infuriated me. I experienced unfathomable outpourings of love and tenderness and fits of rage, often within minutes of each other. New to the heterosexual lifestyle, I had no understanding of any of the rules that exist between men and women. I was clearly a man in the throes of a struggle, attempting to understand what I believed to be God's destiny for my life.

With our engagement, we began the process of deciding where to live, what our wedding invitations would look like, who we should invite, where we should have the wedding and all of the other decisions that heterosexual couples make together before a wedding. While appreciative of the social acceptance, I found the dog pile of decisions overwhelming and quite distracting to the growth of our relationship. Pundit's state that over 40% of marriages end in divorce and with the heap of decisions heaped on top of us this statistic makes complete sense. I thought about eloping with Judy, but she wanted something traditional, so we settled on a Montana wedding in the dead of winter with a honeymoon at Big Mountain in Whitefish, Montana. Judy would rather have traveled to Jamaica but I wasn't ready to celebrate alone with her. We invited the Medora family to our wedding and on our honeymoon so we could celebrate this occasion together — a family of Christ.

WEDDING

(Age 26)

I called Judy's father to ask for her hand in marriage. I hadn't ever met any of Judy's family and without as much as one good wish; he said yes and promptly hung up. It was a stark reminder that my past would not be welcome news, further confirmation for both Judy and me that we should remain silent. Again, it was her choice and although I feared it would be a barrier to the relationship I looked forward to developing with them, it was her family and her decision.

With all of the invitations mailed, our pre-marital counseling complete, a dress borrowed from her good friend Wendy and our six-day skiing honeymoon booked to include the Medora family we flew home in December 1993 to get married. As logical as an engineering equation, I thought it made sense to invite the Medora family to go skiing with us on our honeymoon as they had been our family from the beginning of our journey. The Medoras were the only people on earth who had walked this journey with me from the very first day and I wanted, needed really, them to be there with me as I closed the final chapter on my homosexual lifestyle as I said "I do."

Our rehearsal dinner was one of the most intimate nights of my life. With 20+ guests, Judy and I had taken time to handwrite thank you cards to every single person in attendance. We shared our thoughts, individually and as a couple, as to how each person had impacted our lives. We had prayed over our words, and while the gathered crowd didn't know one another, our words served to bond them together as we broke bread and celebrated our union. One by one every person at the table stood up and spoke from their hearts. It was as if Jesus Christ were seated at the table peeling back the layers of everyone's insecurities and fears. People's hearts bloomed like flowers as they spoke and by the end of the evening handshakes were replaced with hugs.

Unbeknownst to me, my mother had arranged to have fifteen acapella singers serenade us and as Pastor Valentine delivered the dinner prayer, in they walked. There's an old saying that the way to a man's heart is through his stomach. For me, it's music. As they began to sing, I began to weep. Silent tears at first followed by a few choked sobs and then when I could no longer hold back, I buried my head and sobbed. My past came flooding back to me in that moment, all of the contradictions and difficulties, the struggles and accomplishments, the joy of the moment and the fear of the future. So many people at the table, my best man included, had no idea of my private journey and I know my breakdown was somewhat frightening, but I couldn't hold it in. It was the best gift my mother ever gave me and I still get teary eyed when I think of that evening.

I never openly shared my struggle with my family, best man, or anyone else but the Medora family and my Aunt Katy. At that point in my life I didn't have the words to express my hopes, fears, anger or desires for my life. I felt like an island with just a few inhabitants and the sunshine from God above. I had no desire to open myself up to everyone around me and feel their judgment, nor did I have any need to explain myself to those who wondered about my sudden sexual turnaround. I had grown to believe that if I gave in to self-pity or doubt, it would diminish the gift of my example to everyone around me, and my only desire was to glorify God for this gift of marriage to which everyone was a witness. In my eyes, this was a majestic and glorious day that belonged to Christ.

The following evening Judy and I were married at the Clark Fork Christian Center with a reception at the Holiday Inn in downtown Missoula. A snowy night with a bitter cold breeze, it was the perfect setting for an intimate affair. The night had finally arrived where we had planned to make Jesus the center of attention with hand-written vows, praise music and a speech from my spirit-filled Aunt. Judy and I understood people's confusion surrounding our haste to get married, so we did our best to put the attention on Christ. The only person who asked me about my prior lifestyle was my step-brother Greg and, in that moment, I was filled with such hope that I remember telling him my walk was in the hands of God. I believed.

Judy and I cut out of the reception early so we could experience the full blessing of our wedding night. I hadn't been with a woman in over ten years and my first few experiences were lackluster at best, so I was filled with nervous anticipation as we closed the door on our bridal suite. True to form, I had tried to honor God by abstaining from any self-pleasure for the forty days and forty nights prior to our marriage. Since I had no idea if I would be able to perform the consummating act I believed that my sacrificial act to God would serve to ease my fears. As Judy slipped out of her dress, the evening unfolded without a wrinkle and we were — in the eyes of God and everyone in society — husband and wife.

As we arose the next morning, I do not believe that either one of us doubted our sincerity, our collective and individual desire to serve the Lord, or our belief that our marriage would work if we kept faith with God. As one half of a marital union, I felt like the luckiest man alive, and for a few fleeting hours my fear was drowned out by sheer joy. The love, acknowledgment and acceptance of our marriage was so different from the life I had led for the past ten years, it was nearly impossible for me not to feel as if I were walking right next to God.

We spent the next six days bundled up with the Medora family, skiing, playing board games, praying and enjoying the local culture of Montana. Yes, Judy and I had one monster fight in the ski lodge that left us all in gales of laughter, but that's a story for another time.

HUSBAND AND WIFE

(Ages 25 – 28)

Like my life on a submarine, reality hit me as soon as the honeymoon started. Judy and I were now bound together twenty-four hours a day, seven days a week. We found an apartment on Curtis Street in San Diego and tried to settle into the cadence of our life together. I hadn't ever been in a long-term relationship before, let alone with a woman, and my adjustment into married life was a bit like navigating a Montana road in the springtime. I did what I knew best and began working myself at a feverish pace. Up at 5 a.m. to play racquetball, I headed to work routing submarines, ran ten miles at lunch, came home and grabbed a quick dinner and then headed out the door to school, arriving back home at 11 p.m.

In February 1994, a few months after our wedding, the Navy assigned me to become a Drug and Alcohol Counselor at the Counseling and Assistance Center in San Diego. I was a case worker assigned to evaluate the abuse or dependency of alcohol for those military members who had recently had an untoward incident involving alcohol. Under the supervision of a clinical psychologist I worked with another counselor and ran a month-long group therapy process that included goals and objectives for military personnel to complete. It was a complete reversal from every other military assignment I had been assigned. The Counseling and Assistance Center required us to talk about our feelings and fears, and share openly about our lives. It was the only assignment in which I dared to crack the door open on the details of my sexual past and current transition. I never spoke the full truth of my past, but gave enough of myself for those around me to be able to fill in the blanks and understand my desire to lead an authentic life.

Judy continued her work at San Diego Hospice and remained resolutely silent about our marital secret. We spent many nights with her friends playing games, going out for drinks, enjoying dinner and dressing up for costume parties, and yet there was never a moment that Judy wanted to share our secret. Judy's friends allowed me into their circle, but it was clear to me that I would never be given a key to unlock the barrier between us. The guys talked football, the girls talked about the boys and I couldn't relate to any of them. I was still working my twelve step reparative therapy program while working a full-time job and going to school at night. Friendly but not close, that's how my friendship with Judy's friends remained.

Magic Mountain, Disneyland, Harvest Crusade, a baptism for Judy, Promise Keepers, a Barbra Streisand concert, Missoula, Oregon and Las Vegas — our married life unfolded with interpersonal growth and always, with Christ at the center. Much like my previous life, we became a segregated couple with two sets of friends; on one side, the Medoras and extended family who knew our truth, on the other side, everyone else who did not. Church on Sundays, Bible study during the week and secular friendships with Judy — we were split evenly down the middle. It was a source of conflict for us that never went away. Over time I became resentful of the fact that Judy would not share my past with her friends or family. I understood her unwillingness to share my past as a source of shame for her, which caused me to feel "less than" in the human department. She would cajole and prod me to join in the discussions with her male friends, not realizing that it felt as foreign to me as the first day I stepped onto the soil of Bogota, Colombia. I couldn't undo the past 25+ years to make myself into someone else, and Judy didn't appear to want to accept this truth, and so we hobbled along together trying to meet in the middle of our lives.

As our marriage turned the corner and we celebrated our first year anniversary, I could feel my past breathing down my neck. With a packed schedule from 5 a.m. to 11 p.m., I had rationalized my way out of my counseling sessions and dropped out of sight from the reparative group therapy. I had yet to realize that in order for me to stay focused on the present I needed to seek others who understood my past, which I suppose is why AA meetings are so important. I found myself in dangerous territory as I made my way back into reparative therapy.

Year after year, my homosexual desires and thoughts remained steady. They had diminished in the beginning of this process, which I suspected was due to the desperation I felt over the circumstances of Bud and wanting to end my life. With my past now in a different closet, I couldn't seem to escape the steady nag of same-sex sexual desires that met me in every social setting and situation. While I was now able to meet men without sexualizing our encounters, my thoughts still lingered in the men's underwear department when I should have been focused on the ladies lingerie department. True to form, Judy never brought the issue of my same-sex desires to the forefront in private or public, and so I found myself in a different glass cage unable to breathe a word about what I was feeling. Over time I learned to present the "happiest straight man" face to everyone I met, and slowly stopped sharing my struggles with the Medora family as the continuance of my same-sex desires became a source of shame for me, as if I had somehow failed those who believed in me the most.

My walk with God was marred by unanswered questions. By our third year of marriage I felt a sense of anger with the Lord, for He hadn't released me from my own desires. In my mind I had made a deal with God in the parking lot of Body Workshop and while He had held up His end of the bargain by bringing me a wife, I couldn't understand how He expected me to walk with Him if my sexual hunger was pulling me in a different direction. Through the storm of confusion I remained resolutely silent except when I prayed, which was slowly turning more accusatory and much less grateful for my newfound life.

By 1996 Judy and I had been married for close to three years and my assignment as a Drug and Alcohol Counselor was coming to a close along with the completion of my six-year enlistment with the Navy. I had completed my college degree, was an aerobics instructor at several local gyms and wanted to pursue my passion for fitness and quite possibly a PhD in Psychology. I had served the Navy for close to ten years and I believed it was time for me to get out of the service to pursue other options. Typical to form, Judy and I prayed about it at length and decided that I should apply for a PhD program as well as Officer Candidate School which would allow me to become a Naval Officer and stay in the Navy.

For as long as I could remember I had always wanted to wear the uniform of a Naval Officer. I believed I could be an asset to the Navy as an Officer. The other part of me wanted to become a PhD so that I could work with men who were struggling with their sexuality. I understood the dilemma better than anyone else, which included the perils of a military investigation, reparative therapy and now, marriage to a woman. I felt like I had come full circle and while I still wasn't quite sure what my same-sex-desire future held, I continued to hold on to the belief that I was capable of giving back to struggling men to help them understand. Judy, resolute in her silence, wasn't keen on the fact that I wanted to speak out and counsel men who were struggling with their same-sex sexuality. It was a constant source of conflict between us.

Unsure of the future, I submitted my paperwork to Officer Candidate School and several PhD programs. In the meantime I attended several men's retreats, sharing my testimony and speaking out on the topic of re-parative therapy. I never proclaimed complete deliverance from my ho-mosexual past or same-sex feelings, but instead I held on and spoke to the belief that God would someday deliver me from the cross I carried.

A few months later, I received word back from the Navy that I had been accepted to Officer Candidate School to work as a Cryptologic Of-ficer as a uniformed member of the National Security Agency. A first-time candidate, I hadn't expected an acceptance letter to become a Naval Officer and was unaware that a job within the National Security Agency required a Top Secret/Special Compartmentalized Information (TS/SCI) clearance. Unaware of the clearance needs, my boss at the Counseling and Assistance Center, Lieutenant Commander Chancellor, accepted the appointment to Officer Candidate School on my behalf. She called the entire staff to-gether to present me with her Ensign bars — an honored tradition that says to everyone in view she gives her blessing for me to become a Naval Officer.

In June of 1996, two months before I was ordered to report to Offi-cer Candidate School, Lieutenant Commander Chancellor received a mes-sage stating I had been disqualified from attending due to the fact that I was ineligible for a SCI clearance. Although Christ had forgiven me for my past transgressions, it appeared that the military investigation had one last judgment to put upon my life, as I had been denied a Special Com-partmentalized Information clearance several years prior — a fact that had slipped my mind.

DON'T ASK, DON'T TELL
(Age 28)

Slated to begin Officer Candidate School in Pensacola, Florida on August 10, 1996, I was informed I was ineligible in June, just eight weeks prior to my scheduled start date – due to my ineligibility status for an SCI clearance. With the clock moving faster than any bureaucratic process I had ever seen, I either had to get this issue cleared up or lose my appointment to Officer Candidate School and head back to the submarine force as an enlisted man. With a college degree in hand, I no longer wanted to serve within the enlisted ranks as I had set my sights on Officer Candidate School. The urgency for resolution was great.

The denial of my clearance forced me once again to divulge every secret of my past to Lieutenant Commander Chancellor. I had to share the investigative history, the details of the polygraph exam and interviews, the psychologist's report and the denial of my SCI clearance. Although I had spoken in code about my private life to my fellow Drug and Alcohol counselors, opening up to a Naval Officer was dangerous territory. With my history in her hands, and no idea of her moral position surrounding a "suspected homosexual" investigation, it was well within her power to drag her feet towards the finish line of resolution, which would have ended my military officer dreams.

Shame, dread, anger and remorse rose up within me as I left Lieutenant Commander Chancellor's office. Having spilled every last detail of my investigation like a hot cup of coffee in our laps left me feeling deflated once again. I was forced to divulge the indiscretions of my past to a woman who knew my wife, who had put her faith in me to become a Naval Officer, and now I had turned her world upside down with a story of my sordid past. Was I the person she thought I was? Did she really know me like she thought she had? Did she make a mistake in recommending me for Officer Candidate School? Up until this point I had the appearance of a squeaky-clean enlisted man; married, hard-working, college graduate, always ranked near the top of the evaluation process and now . . . a bomb. As I got into my car to head back home I realized the gravity of this situation.

My shame, dread and remorse turned into a fireball of anger. I had been in and out of reparative therapy, had surrendered my life to God and believed He had delivered a wife who could support my transition from homo to heterosexuality. Would I never be able to escape discrimination? I felt I had worked ten times harder than any of my peers, proving to myself and everyone around me that I was indeed worthy of achievement. Where, I wondered, was the justice in this archaic military system?

With my story back out in the open, I had to have a face-to-face meeting with Lieutenant Espinosa, the security officer for the Naval Base, and recount every single detail of the investigation so he could draft an appropriate message to the Department of the Navy Central Adjudication Facility, asking them to re-adjudicate my SCI clearance eligibility. I was now four weeks away from my scheduled departure to Officer Candidate School and with every day that passed it appeared that God had a different plan for my life. The problem was I had already turned down a few colleges and made preparations to leave for Florida.

President Bill Clinton had signed the "Don't Ask, Don't Tell" law into effect on December 21, 1993. I had heard about the law and understood that we were scheduled to receive mandatory training on this issue, but I suppose like every other heterosexual male I didn't believe that this new piece of legislation applied to me. I wasn't living an openly-gay lifestyle, I was married and while I knew it would probably benefit a lot of other people, I really didn't care. I was too busy going to college to finish my degree, working through my own reparative therapy program and trying to make my marriage work. While I had homosexual desires and attractions, to the rest of the world I was just another married man living out his life, and so I worked to ignore all homosexual issues including legislation that I believed wasn't relevant to me.

With my SCI clearance denied, I went home, fired up my computer and read the newly- approved policy of Don't Ask, Don't Tell. The basic premise of this policy is that it prohibits people who "demonstrate a propensity or intent to engage in homosexual acts" from serving in the armed forces of the United States because their presence "would create an unacceptable risk to the high standards of morale, good order and discipline, and unit cohesion." Military personnel could not disclose their sexual orientation nor could they speak about homosexual relationships while serving in the military. If service members chose to disclose their homosexual orientation, they could be separated.

The policy seemed as silly to me as stating that a person could have black skin, but as long as they kept white paint on them at all times, not showing anyone their true color, they could continue to serve within the military. I believe people are either born gay or born straight — just like skin color — so not disclosing it forced everyone into a segregated mindset. I hadn't denied my sexuality, I was attempting to work through it, and I understood all too well that I was a homosexual male attempting to work through a reparative therapy process so I could lead a heterosexual lifestyle. Barring a miracle from God, I knew that I would always be a homosexual male attempting to walk with Christ in a heterosexual lifestyle. This new policy had more circular reasoning than a hula-hoop. Service members could not discriminate against closeted homosexuals — huh? If a person is closeted, how can they be discriminated against? Angry from having to discuss my past, I felt even angrier towards this new policy. It seemed to put homosexual service members in a no-win situation.

Back to work and seething mad, I asked to be removed as a counselor within my group therapy process as this current hurdle had forced the sensitivity towards others right out of me. The ridiculousness of the military policies had negatively affected my work performance. Back in my office, I spent the next several weeks interviewing new clients and following up on existing college applications for a PhD program. I was sick and tired of the bullshit with my security clearance and I remember telling Judy that no matter what the Navy decided I was going to get out and go get my PhD. At last . . . I had reached the point where I was ready to leave the Navy on my terms.

It took two and half weeks for the Department of the Navy Central Adjudication Facility to make a final ruling on my SCI clearance. Lieutenant Commander Chancellor called me into her office and told me to go get my jacket and cover (hat) as we were going to take a trip over to Lieutenant Espinosa's office to receive the news of my adjudicated case. I was angry and nervous all in the same moment as she drove us over to his office. I was asked to be seated in the hallway. Within about ten minutes I was called into the office and told to have a seat. Lieutenant Commander Chancellor reached across the desk and put her hand out. I wasn't sure what she was doing, so I grasped her hand and she looked me dead in the eye and told me that I had just overcome my first hurdle as an Officer Candidate. The Department of the Navy Central Adjudication Facility had ruled in my favor. Due to the "Don't Ask, Don't Tell" policy, I was now eligible for a full TS/SCI clearance and could become a Cryptologic Officer for the National Security Agency.

As we rode back to our office building together I remember Lieutenant Commander Chancellor telling me that as a Naval Officer I would be faced with many challenges; challenges that would appear insurmountable. She told me that it was my job to look the problem directly in the eye and find a solution. I could no longer ask to be excused from my duties, no matter how difficult the task or heavy the burden. Her words reverberated in my mind for the next twelve years.

BECOMING A CRYPTOLOGIC OFFICER

(Ages 28 - 29)

Just like coffee ice cream, Officer Candidate School isn't for everyone. For me it was a delicious taste of freedom from my marriage, reparative therapy and the heavy burden of my sexual transition. I was in one hundred percent lock-down for the first four weeks in which I wasn't allowed to look at my food, was forced to drink eight glasses of water per meal and memorize "Anchors Aweigh," the "Marine's Hymn," the six articles of the Code of Conduct, the Sailor's Creed, the eleven General Orders of a Sentry, the fourteen people in my Chain of Command, the entire Navy military rank structure broken down into collar device, shoulder board and sleeve insignia, the entire Marine Corps Officer rank structure, the Navy enlisted rank structure, the phonetic alphabetic A-Z, and the fourteen leadership traits. It was the first time in over four years that I was able to quiet my mind and focus on something other than my sexual conundrum.

Officer Candidate School is one of the only places on earth where sex does not exist. You are constipated for the first week or two, you have to maintain a 1,000 yard stare at all times, you can only speak if you ask permission, which of course is impossible because you lose your voice from screaming about the fourth day after you arrive –- and you are so sleep deprived that nothing looks good. You are given ten minutes a day to take a shit, shower and shave –- and you must accomplish all of that with 40+ other guys trying to do the same thing, at the same time, with three shower heads, ten sinks and ten toilets. Unlike enlisted Boot Camp where the guy above me was jacking off so hard I thought he was going to dislodge our bunk beds and come crashing down on top of me, Officer Candidate School is nothing to wiggle your arm at.

Reveille was at 5:00 a.m. We had to be standing at attention on a black line in the hallway at 5:10 a.m. Off to exercise, then to eat, back to shower, off to class, then to eat, back to class and then outside for rifle drills and marching exercises until it's time for dinner. You move as one, like a giant caterpillar rolling down the sidewalk in and out of buildings. You aren't an individual, you are an Officer Candidate, and you belong to one Drill Instructor –- and one alone. You are his un-hatched butterfly and it's his goal to test you beyond what you thought possible and then some.

Push-ups in the sand, on the sidewalk and in the middle of the street, my deflated chest became two chiseled hunks of meat. Jumping jacks on the lawn, in front of the chow hall, in the middle of traffic -- anywhere the Drill Instructor feels like "dropping" you for being a lazy pig, he will, and he does. You are forced to ask permission to speak, permission to go to the bathroom and permission to do anything you aren't told to do. Asking doesn't guarantee a positive response, so I learned to take a piss every chance I got whether I had to go or not.

One of my favorite memories is a blistering hot day where we found ourselves outside marching with rifles, getting ready for our drill competition. We were at an event which required our entire class to march with precision, conducting rifle movements while other Drill Instructors watched and gave us a class grade which had the potential to put a flag of success on top of our flagpole. Flags equaled recognition, for it meant that your officer class had passed a myriad of events and learned to work as a team. Unfortunately, one of the members of our team was given two left feet and an inability to swing a rifle around while walking. As the Drill Instructor ran beside our moving caterpillar, this young man swung his rifle and hit the Drill Instructor in the face. For the next forty-five minutes our entire class performed eight count body builders (jumping jack, jump to the push-up position, push up, and jump back up again), while this young man watched. Twenty minutes into our punishment, this young man broke down in tears while the Drill Instructor refused to let him participate. We had to pay for his sins, and we paid while he watched. That was a turning point for our class, and a day I almost quit.

Towards the eighth week of Officer Candidate School I found myself out with my classmates giving new definition to the word freedom. I no longer had to wonder if in a swarm of caterpillars they would discover that I was a mosquito in a butterfly costume. For that brief period of time, I believed that I was a butterfly and I had just broken free from the cocoon of Officer Candidate School. My sexuality a distant memory behind the rigors I had just accomplished, I drank like nobody was watching and danced like a real brother on Soul Train. My dad, his wife Cindy and Judy all came out to Florida to watch me graduate and pin on my new officer rank — Ensign Tripp.

In the nine months I was assigned in Florida, it was the only time Judy came out to see me. During Officer Candidate School Judy couldn't visit, but when I graduated and moved over to the Cryptologic Division Officer Course to learn about the life and duties of a Cryptologic Officer, she could have joined me to live in the Officer Barracks just like every other wife. Instead, she stayed back in Oregon with her family. I had received orders to the Naval Security Group Activity in Rota, Spain and she was determined to spend every single last minute with her family in Oregon. Now that we're speaking the truth, I have a little confession about my tour in Spain. I was given a choice between a job in the United States and a job overseas, and it was my decision to go to Spain. Having lived in South America, I wanted to experience the Spanish culture and life in Spain and I knew that if I asked Judy she would have told me that she didn't want to live overseas, which is exactly what she told me after I accepted my military orders. I had just worked my ass off in Officer Candidate School and was getting ready to work my ass off again in the Cryptologic Division Officer Course. I made the decision to move to Spain and I didn't consult God, or Judy. I wanted out of America and away from my past.

Struggling with being alone in Pensacola after just accomplishing a major life goal, I drank a full cup of resentment every morning when I woke up at 5 a.m. to go running and by nighttime my indigestion was so strong that I had no other choice but to head out to the local bars for antacids named cute, cuter and downright sexy. Listen up ladies, because I'm only going to say this once:. if your husband tells you on your third date that he struggles with his sexuality and you work a "homosexual reparative therapy" course together, get married and he then goes off to a military boot camp for thirteen weeks and comes out looking all buff, rough and tumble, don't give him a "high five" and go back to what's convenient for you while he continues to work his ass off to support the family. Take care of your man, upside down and inside out because if you don't someone else is going to put him in the hot spin cycle of the dryer and press those sheets for you.

Muscular, slim and looking every shade of erotic, I was a superstar student by day and a homeless vagrant man by night. With no wife at my side, I defined the motto "work hard, play harder" and true to form, my military brothers hung with me through rock and roll bowling, house parties at the beach, crazy nights downtown and drinking games in the barracks. Our days consisted of morning runs, school house fun, evening puns and a ton of studying. When I wasn't cracking the books or beers with my brothers I was out walking over the cracks of my sexual identity, back in the throes of contradiction and confusion. Alone, in a city where I knew no one and where the reminder of my past was filled with nothing but good memories, I began the struggle to understand my sexuality with renewed intensity.

I became the definition of schizophrenic in every sense of the word. Defined as a "straight married man" to Judy's family and our mutual friends, a "gay married man" to some of my family and friends, and a "straight, married military officer" according to all of my military brothers and sisters with whom I never spoke a word of my double life. I continued to mask my conflicted relationships through overachieving; a shooting star who distracted viewers from the darkness in my heart. I had become the guy who thought he could do anything; anything but conquer his homosexual desires. Accomplishments and accomplishing everything I set out to achieve professionally was the only way I was able to make any sense out of my life.

Like a steam engine, I too needed a release from the reality and fantasy of my lives — a chance to let all the balls drop on the floor while I fondled my own. In those sacred and fleeting moments I assumed the identity of a freelance writer, just in town for a few nights or weeks, writing stories about the local culture while I got to know a few of the local men. No real name and a made-up identity, I didn't seek sex as much as I sought understanding. To be able to walk into a gay bar and feel laughter, longing, sadness, craving and raw sexual tension was as shocking as peeing on an electric fence. Overcome by the feeling, my mind was unsure of how to turn around and walk back out the door, so I continued forward toward dance beats and Bud Lights. In those rare nights when I summoned the courage to expose myself, the burden of existing in triplicate became so heavy that sometimes I told my story to a complete stranger, if only to unpack my burden on to someone else. A part of me hoped that my words would expose the truth, causing me to be caught and caged. I began to wonder if my life wouldn't be better without resistance -- just a sweet surrender of knowing that the end had arrived.

On January 23, 1997 I drove back to Naval Air Station Pensacola after a night of pure escape; Whitney Houston carving out old memories in my heart as a full moon danced on the water. The trees along the water's edge filled the banks and I wondered what kind of peace must reside inside their limbs. I envisioned taking my last breath there, a place where my dream of becoming a Naval Officer had blossomed. In that moment I could feel the coolness of the ground wafting towards my feet as I hung swaying from above, knowing that my mind would no longer have to play in three different worlds while my soul played in one. Was I bound to a world that I did not physically live in? I looked whole, but I wasn't even half — just one third of a person in each regard, trying to honor each one as if I were one hundred percent whole. I wondered what stopped me from giving myself away fully to the breathing human being that was my wife. Why couldn't I feel her passion inside of me like the hot breath of a man on my neck, in my loins and suffocating my inner desires? I wanted to crave her like I craved the stubble of a man's beard, the strength of his fingers between mine and the power that lies between his legs, but I never did. Crossing through the gate, I went back to the barracks alone – yet again.

With my time in Pensacola coming to a close my table for two was folded up by a drag queen cocktail waitress in downtown Pensacola. All I ever shared with my dinner companions was conversation. I wanted their dessert, but couldn't quite muster up the courage to place an order. Some were struggling with God and sexuality, and together we had meal after meal of robust flavorful words but always stopped short of partaking in the sugary sweetness of passion. Reminds me of a guy I knew once, a man named Chuck. He killed himself with a gun and a plastic bag wrapped around his head.

Chuck didn't give you the impression that he was the kind of guy who would kill himself. I met him in the winter of 1987 -- a cocky, blond-haired, brown-eyed, cowboy-boot-and-wrangler-wearing little bull dog. There he was, outside on the patio holding court with about five or six people, demanding attention and manipulating the conversation to meet his insatiable desires. The only reason I went over to the table was to say goodbye to one of the people listening to his holiness. My first instinct was to walk over and slap the fuck and arrogance right out of him. Laughing like a hyena, he turned his attention to me as I approached. A self-righteous remark, laughter and then an invitation to sit down –– that's how I met Chuck.

For the next ten years, as a single gay man and then as a married man struggling through reparative therapy, Chuck remained one of my best friends. We fought like two sisters, argued like opposing politicians, pushed our personal agendas like drug dealers and loved one another like brothers. Chuck was the only guy I could sleep with, my hard on pressing into his back and his dick hard in my hand, spooning like conjoined twins while we chattered on about nothingness. He was my brother, and my sister. He sold me my first car, a smoking black Ford Thunderbird, that had smoke pouring out of it on the fourteenth day after I purchased it. Chuck not only sold me a smoking car, but somehow managed to convince me I looked smoking hot as Ginger, from Gilligan's Island, as he put on the face and hair of Barbra Streisand. My one and only time in drag, I left the house feeling like a man and came back a harried, drunken sexpot. Drag? The only thing I "dragged" was Marlboro Lights, and Chuck was always on my ass to give those up, unless of course he wanted one.

No doubt, Chuck was trouble –– one of those too smart for his own good kind of guys. He was smart enough to know better and had just enough sprinkle of daredevil to make him look life in the face and laugh. The July fourth weekend of 1989 Chuck and I laughed our way from Norfolk, Virginia to Washington DC. We drove up in Chuck's Fiat –– the noisiest car on earth –– to a hotel in a neighborhood called DuPont Circle. It was my first foray into the forest of DC gay life. Hotel keys secured in our front pockets, Chuck led me around from bar to bar; Southern Comfort pouring down my throat, providing me a great deal of comfort. Somehow we found our way back to the hotel with a distinguished, handsome man. Chuck convinced him that we were airline pilots and just as Chuck began throttling down the runway with Mr. Distinguished, I had to takeoff to the bathroom as the room was spinning out of control. Next thing I knew, the hotel manager was unlocking the bathroom door and Chuck was screaming something about my inability to control myself after countless Southern Comfort cocktails. I'd completely blown Chuck's plan to roll, pitch and yaw with Mr. Handsome -- and he never let me forget it.

I was married and feeling secure in my new lifestyle when Chuck called me in 1994 to break his news.. He was HIV positive. This was the guy who wore rubber gloves and used bleach to clean his kitchen, bathroom and hallway closet. HIV positive, Chuck? He was all bark, no bite, and definitely no sucking and swallowing without dental dams.

I didn't recognize him as I stepped into the main terminal of his regional airport in 1997. The disease, now raging as full blown AIDS, had raped Chuck's face, body and handshake. A ghost of the man I knew, he was bald, frail and unsteady. The devil looked me right in the eye as I stared at the skeleton of one of my best friends from a life lived so long ago. Yes, I had told Judy about Chuck so she knew who he was, but it was impossible for her to understand what he was to me. A gay brother, a man who struggled with his sexuality as much as I, and yet his life took such a different path. His story unraveled as we sat on the hotel room bed.

Faithful boyfriend in DC, a good job, his born again Christian family starting to accept his sexuality — everything was falling into place for Chuck. What he didn't know was that his boyfriend was having random sex every place he could and in the process, gave Chuck the bug, like a cockroach served in between a piece of meatloaf. He had no idea because, in his words, he had finally learned how to trust. Trust, a five letter word just like penis or shaft -- he got both and then the dreaded HIV diagnosis.

A few months after Judy and I moved to Spain I got a phone call telling me that Chuck had killed himself. In his last few months he went to live with an old queen who took compassion on him, and gave him a room and the backyard garden to tend. Typical Chuck, he pulled all of the weeds that Saturday morning, then wrapped his head in a plastic bag, wrote a note and pulled the trigger that ended his life. I sobbed like a schoolgirl when I hung up the phone. Judy came rushing into the kitchen, and I rushed out the backdoor, the contradiction of my life too heavy to explain.

I thought of Chuck as I boarded the plane out of Pensacola on my way to meet Judy at the airport in North Carolina where we headed down to Jamaica for the wedding of one of my newest military friends. Lieutenant and Mrs. Chris A. had lived together in the Officer Barracks in Pensacola while Chris attended the Cryptologic Course with me. Chris and Amy had also received orders to Spain and although Judy had never met them, I was sure she would like them as much as I did.

We arrived in Jamaica amidst a whirlwind of wedding activities. Chris had asked me to be a groomsman, and I couldn't have been more honored. I did the honors of introducing Judy to Chris and Amy and less than twenty-four hours later Judy had made up her mind that she couldn't honor my friendship with them. Time had clearly not caused our hearts to grow fonder and I was immediately resentful of her judgment. From my viewpoint, she had acted with her own self-interest in mind when she chose to stay in Oregon with her family for the entire duration of my schooling in Florida so I didn't believe she was entitled to pass judgment on this new relationship. We were all moving to Spain together where Chris and I would serve as Naval Officers and I was panicked that Judy's stance would sever my relationship with Chris and Amy and quite possibly my position as a brand new officer.

Although I didn't tell Judy, my housing circumstances in Pensacola and the awkward situation with Chris and Amy in Jamaica changed my heart. As we boarded the plane for Spain I couldn't help wonder if this wasn't the beginning of the end for Judy and me. With our carry-on bags securely stored in the overhead we sat down, fastened our seat belts and stared straight ahead, not a single word of prayer between us.

SPAIN

(Ages 29 - 30)

We landed in Spain with the previous nine months of separation a pregnant pause in our relationship. I had been working to achieve success so we could move our lives forward while Judy was back home lamenting her future move across the ocean. Judy had a chip on her shoulder as big as the suitcases we carried from the airport and into the car of our military sponsor. Tension filled the air as we were led to the officer barracks where we stayed for several weeks as I started my new job and Judy looked for housing with one of the officer wives. I wanted to live within the local economy to experience all of the scents wafting from the local culture, but Judy chose a home on base where we would be forced to live with all of the other American military officers. Yellow stucco, manicured yards, a carport for our newly-purchased Toyota Corolla and all of the gossiping a person could handle. It felt like a death sentence.

Within six weeks of arrival I was sent out of the country with two days' notice on an assignment that lasted for close to eight weeks. I wasn't allowed to tell Judy anything about my job, where I was going or what I would be doing. All she knew was that I was leaving, and it was up to her to get our house in order and start a life for herself. This is a pattern that repeated itself several times over the next year; home for a short duration, gone for a short duration, and work hours that caused me to be away from home for extended periods of time. I was a brand new Naval Officer and I knew that in order to make any kind of positive impression, I would have to work my ass off like never before, taking every single assignment thrown my way. That is exactly what I did.

When I was home in Spain the tension between Judy and me was palatable. There were social events, invitations to officer functions and mandatory functions that required both of us to participate. Pomp and circumstance became our middle names with gatherings to welcome new officers, say goodbye to departing officers, and celebrate promotions, retirements, and the accomplishments of every single officer I served with. Invitations from the Commanding Officer weren't truly invitations. They were mandatory events that required both of us to participate, socialize, and celebrate the success of our Naval Command as a cohesive group of people.

Unlike Chris and Amy, Judy chose to stand on the opposite side of the fence when it came to attending any of the social events where my presence was required. Judy didn't like any of the spouses, she didn't like the gatherings and she made it known on several occasions that she didn't want to go. I, on the other hand, had no choice. As an officer I was bound by a sense of duty and I had to create the best possible impression I could. A military officer's spouse has a great deal of influence in setting the right impression, for she was also representing "me" within the social circles of the other officer spouses. Unfortunately, the impression she made became crystal clear to me when the Executive Officer called me into his office one day and asked me if the other wives had done something to offend Judy because she wouldn't return phone calls or attend gatherings to which she was invited.

Judy became a donkey, with her heels dug in so deep that even she couldn't get unstuck. I felt a tremendous sense of resentment toward her as I viewed her stubbornness to participate as an act of sabotage on my career. Had we been stationed within the United States, she might have been able to get away with her lack of desire to participate, but in Spain where the only thing we had was work and social events, it was painfully obvious to every single officer and their spouse that Judy was not a team player.

I attempted to understand the sacrifices that Judy had made when she left her job in San Diego, all of her friends and everything familiar to her – an adjustment that wasn't easy for either of us. I knew that her inability to work and the loss of her friends was taking a mental toll on her and she made that abundantly clear every night when I came home from work. With little patience for anything but work I tried to encourage her by using examples of how the other military wives had adjusted over time, a comparison I should have never used, for it only caused her greater anxiety and anger.

With my continued deployments and the tension mounting faster than a heap of Marines running up a mountain, Judy announced she wanted a baby. A baby had never been a part of the equation we discussed when we decided to get married. I had made it crystal clear to Judy that I had no desire to have any children for I couldn't seem to reconcile my past, and I wasn't capable of working through the details of my life while working full-time and struggling with the cross of my sexuality. A child was absolutely, one hundred percent out of the question, and she knew that. She accepted that fact on the day we said "I do," so her complete reversal took me by storm.

Did I want a child? No. Did I have any desire to be a father? None. I knew I could love another human being, but I didn't believe I had the emotional capacity to deal with the dependency of a human life while my own life seemed to be nothing but hard work and stress. Although I had been able to keep the ghosts of my homosexual past at an arm's length during Officer Candidate School and in Spain due to my constant deployments, I wasn't ready to add another ingredient to the mix of our marriage. My homosexual feelings hadn't diminished and were now haunting me day and night.

In an attempt to assuage Judy's homesickness, her hatred of life in Spain and her resentment for having to give up her job and friends in San Diego, I did what every good husband does and I gave into her request. One singular Sunday morning when she told me she was ovulating she asked me to come into the bedroom. With a sex life as sporadic as her attendance at officer social functions, I satisfied her request and completed the task at hand. Feeling unsupported and betrayed, I'm still not sure why I gave in that fateful morning. I suppose a part of me wanted to keep our relationship alive, but another part of me wanted nothing to do with her anymore.

The singular event that fateful Sunday morning was the event that changed the course of our lives together. Judy was pregnant. She was overjoyed by the news, and I became depressed. I immediately sought the help of a counselor, and together we began marriage counseling. The news of her pregnancy had caused an emotional earthquake in my life that made me lose my grip on the foundation I had built. We went to see Chaplain Scott, a military priest who could offer help, but not share the contents of our conversation.

Judy and I opened up to Chaplain Scott. I spilled my entire history like a big huge breath that I had been holding inside for years. I spoke of my childhood, I spoke of my sexual conundrum, I spoke of temptation, and I spoke about our marriage. While I have no doubt that Chaplain Scott meant well, the only words I remember him speaking aloud were, "When you walk into a room and see a man you are attracted to, look the other way and pray." Look the other way, look the other way, and look the other way. If I were to look the other way every single time I found a man who I thought was attractive I was better off blind. Judy, embarrassed by the fact that I had openly discussed my sexual secret offered no support.

With a military chaplain attempting to offer guidance on a sexual issue that was forbidden in uniform, I was once again stuck between a rock, and a rock. There was no such thing as a reparative therapy program in Spain, and at this point in my life I had serious doubts about the validity of the program itself. My same-sex desires had never diminished and while I had a better understanding of how to relate to other men, I was still a homosexual male white knuckling my way through life. I felt like God had failed me, reparative therapy had failed me and I was slowly beginning to fail myself in my promise to love my wife until death do us part.

Three months before Judy was to give birth, I was sent out on another assignment where neither the telephone nor internet were available. Two weeks after my departure, Judy went into labor and was mandated to bed rest for the remainder of her pregnancy. Laid up in our house, Amy A. and Judy's good friend, Fern, came over to help. These two ladies provided her twenty-four hour care while I was caring for the security of our country. I arrived home on a Sunday. Twenty-four hours later our son was born.

AUSTIN

(Ages 29 - 31)

As I stood in the delivery room and watched Judy struggle to give birth to our son, something magical happened inside me. The angst of my world burst open into sobs of joy as Austin came into the world. Pink, slimy and two huge lungs, he screamed a big hello to Judy and me as we watched the nurses suction and clean him off. Delivered and wrapped up into a bundle of joy, Austin had arrived.

I stayed home for a few days with Judy as we made our way through learning how to operate a breast pump, car seat, and the myriad of gadgets that had invaded our home. A blanket, bottles, bouncy chair and more binky's than a Macy's department store, our house was filled with all of the creature comforts Austin needed. Our Bible study group and the officers' wives had been more than generous to the two of us; an unexpected surprise indeed.

Austin's arrival had somehow washed away the bitterness that had built up around the edges of my heart and by the time I was required to go back to work I had a difficult time saying goodbye to the little fella. Our routine in place, I would work a full day, come home and strip off my uniform, and then take care of Austin while Judy headed off to the gym. It was important for me to spend alone time with Austin and I also knew that Judy needed a break from the constant responsibility. With bottles and blankets, Austin and I managed together a few short hours a day.

With Austin finally sleeping through the night, the tension in my relationship with Judy escalated to the point that neither one of us could sleep. We were fighting constantly and neither one of us could see the vantage point of the other. If I tried to give my input on how Austin should be raised, Judy proceeded with her plan of action as if she hadn't heard me. She reminded me that she was the mother and the primary caretaker, while I reminded her I was the breadwinner. The softness between us had melted away, replaced by a steely cold demeanor. God was nowhere to be found.

With the pending wedding of Judy's best friend, Lynn, a woman who was kind but cool towards me, Judy, Austin and I flew back to America in September 1998. As we landed in San Diego, the Medora family greeted us at the airport pouring their spirit-filled love all over the three of us. Time seemed to stand still as we gathered in their home for several days of fellowship and prayer. It was the first time that Judy and I had prayed together in over six months. Awkward and somewhat clumsy, we made our way to Lynn and Tim's wedding, calling a truce between our warring camps. From San Diego we flew up to Oregon and then over to Montana to show off our newest addition to the family. It was a trip that highlighted the tension-filled gap between Judy and me as my sister took our picture under a tree, showing us exactly how miserable we both were.

Back in Spain, the matador and the bull faced off against one another back in the ring of marital discord. Judy had become close friends with a pilot's wife in Spain, a woman with a hidden agenda. Every single time her presence graced our doors I could see the judgment emanating from her eyes. While Judy swore she hadn't divulged my past to her, I could tell that I had been made out to be the bad guy in our relationship. Many nights I came home to an empty house with Judy and Austin off on a walk or over to Fern's house for dinner. With no welcome, I began to realize that I was no longer welcome in my own home.

In March of 1999 I was asked to attend a military meeting in Pensacola. I was only too happy to escape my tension-filled house in Spain. Judy and I were at each other's throats clawing for control and understanding. I didn't know what else she wanted, but I knew I couldn't give any more than I had already given her. Work had been especially challenging, my new rank forcing me to spread my new wings of authority in unfamiliar ways. No longer an enlisted man, the new challenges of responsibility were more daunting than I had expected and with the war that was raging in my home life, Pensacola was a welcome reprieve.

Back in Florida where I had spent so much time alone, I managed to escape from the evening's social gatherings and found myself back in a smoke-filled bar. A Bud Light in one hand and a cigarette in the other, the rumbling and raspy tones of Madonna beckoned me to join her and dance once again, with unabashed pleasure. Men with men, women with women, and every variation in between, my heart knew the answer to my heartache.

As I boarded the 747 to head back to Spain I remember feeling a sense of tremendous dread and relief. I was filled with anger towards God because He hadn't quelled my homosexual desires and convinced that the life I was living was filled with so many contradictions that I wasn't sure I was even fulfilling His will. I sat in my airplane seat and prayed and thought and prayed some more. By the time I touched down in Spain, I believed I had my answer.

DIVORCE

(Age 31)

As I opened the front door, silence rushed up and put its arms around me. Judy and Austin were not home. I was eighty-five percent sure of what I needed to do, but unsure of how to proceed. I had heaped mountains of guilt upon myself about being gay, heaps of guilt as I worked through reparative therapy and added more guilt after I was married because I didn't believe that I was somehow "man" enough for Judy. As a gay man I had never quite felt gay enough in a gay bar and straight enough in a straight bar. As a married man I had always felt as if Judy's vow of silence with her friends and family was somehow a silent indicator of her own private shame about my circumstances. After so many years of working through my sexuality, I knew I could not change. My sexual preference was biologic, and in no way was it a choice.

With Judy back at home, our fighting began again in earnest. As our voices escalated, Austin began pushing his lawn mower in circles. As we yelled and screamed, I could see his behavior change, and that was the singular defining moment for me when I knew for sure I wanted a divorce. I have no tolerance for child abuse and I considered our fighting to be a form of mental abuse towards Austin. I had lived through enough yelling and screaming to know the funny feeling that punches you in the stomach and makes you wonder if the world is coming to an end. At barely a year old, Austin was exhibiting the same behavior that I knew all too well, and with that I spoke the words aloud.

We had threatened divorce many times over the past year, but this time I knew I wanted out. I no longer wanted the "actor" part of being a straight man in a gay man's body. I no longer wanted to feel shame about who I was as a person, or wonder about the shame that Judy felt. For one last final time, I was willing to become the son of a bitch and state I wanted a divorce so I could let myself and Judy off the hook of our commitment together.

In May of 1999 I flew back to Montana to celebrate my father's sixtieth birthday, and that was the last time Judy and I were together as husband and wife. Before I left we took an inventory of everything we owned together and laid out custody of those items, and notarized it with the base legal counsel. Judy promised me she would never touch my military retirement, ask for my retirement, or seek legal assistance in acquiring it. What I understood to be an iron clad agreement between the two of us, signed by an attorney, was a mistake for which I will never forgive myself:

July 17th, 1999 Journal Entry: As I sit here and look at this blank screen I feel as if I am looking at the ocean's horizon with no paddle boat, no life jacket and no sign of rescue in sight — dog paddling my way to survival. Judy left on the 6th of June 1999 with Austin, while I was in Montana. I came home to Spain, an empty house that Judy didn't bother to lock before she left, and drank red wine until it drowned out the howling cries of inequity I felt inside. It all seems so unfair to me. A gay man trying to get married in order to fit in, accepting the religious truth that my feelings were a sin, and now facing the reality that my feelings aren't going to go away. I have lost my dreams, a friend, a confidant, and a son. I white knuckled my way through a heterosexual life for seven years, no support from any gay entities, and now I am back on another roller coaster, white knuckling my way to a reality undetermined. When will the next turn come? From what direction will I be thrown about like a limp rag doll accepting his fate? I am not going to listen to anyone tell me that I need to turn this way or that, or if I close my eyes and just take the ride the pain will go away. I can't paddle upstream anymore, I can't do it — I just can't. I don't know what that means for me or where my feelings will take me, but I can't pretend anymore.

This is liberating and yet painful. I long for the normalcy that my relationship with Judy brought. I miss the tranquility, the quiet days, the tender hugs. I don't miss the internal battle — the loss I am now experiencing because I failed to win that battle. I drew the sword and cut the ties for I knew that it was causing Judy more pain than she deserved. We were both dying inside and too scared or ashamed to reach out. So, now I will deal with that shame and try to make some sense of it. I have cried a mountain of tears today. I have wailed, wept, and paced around the house calling out for help. I cannot turn to anyone, for my words have repercussions far beyond their spoken value. I have a military career in Spain which is my life's blood and I can't throw it away by speaking out about my homosexuality. In this turbulent time I will ride this wave because I know the dips and turns of the Navy, and I can survive it. I can't cut off all of my support systems. Where would I go?

With Judy and Austin back in America my work days overflowed into nights and sometimes mornings. Alone in Spain, struggling to connect the dots of my sexuality once again, my emotional circuits were on overload.

The only friend Judy made in Spain, the pilot's wife with whom she spent all of her time before she left, turned me in to the base housing authorities as I wasn't allowed to live as a "bachelor" in military officer housing. Still married by law, the pilot's wife threw a stink bomb that convinced the housing authority I was single and I was forced to move out into the local economy. We had agreed that Judy would get the car, so I had no choice but to buy another car. I purchased a rusted yellow, push-button start, 1978 Ford Fiesta. A broken spirit, car and home life — thoughts of suicide offered me unequaled solace once again. I was inconsolable, a madman whose anger threatened to choke my breath as I chugged bottle after bottle of red wine. Chris and Amy A., my two best friends in Spain, brought me tissues, wine and their support as they helped me move out into town.

As our divorce proceedings got underway, Judy hired a divorce attorney in Oregon, to represent her. Stuck in Spain, I had no attorney and couldn't use the legal counsel on base as we had visited them together and they could no longer represent my sole interests. I tried calling Judy several times to discuss this matter, but between the time difference and her disinterest, I was only able to reach her a few times. As we spoke, I assumed we were speaking the truth, until I got a letter a few hours after we had hung up the phone. Judy's attorney was going after my military retirement, full custody, alimony and a whopping monthly child support payment. Incensed I picked up the phone and called her back; two weeks later I was given notice that I was harassing my wife and was to have no further contact until the divorce was finalized.

The final blow came when I went home to visit my son. Judy's parents forbid me from entering the house and her brother-in-law told me that homosexuals weren't welcome on their property. I believed Judy had betrayed me in the worst possible way. She told her family and friends that the reason we were getting divorced was because I had told her I was gay after we got married.

She had known since our third date.

FRANCE
(Age 31)

With my home on the military base in Spain now a part of my past, I rented an apartment in Rota that was situated on a narrow curve of road, making it impossible to drive by and look in. Visible, yet difficult to see inside, it was the perfect analogy for my life. The smell of hope erased, suicide was the only scent the neighbor dog could smell wafting from my kitchen. A knife, a rope, and an innocuous bottle of aspirin -- I held them in my hands nightly while contemplating my future.

Routine was my friend, and I was nothing if not a man of routine. Up at 5 a.m., to work by 5:45 a.m., chewing on numbers and formulas until lunch, outside to the greasy spoon cafe, and then back to my desk for a dessert of spreadsheets and problem solving. My goal was a 4 p.m. departure when my 1978 Ford Fiesta would wiggle me home, and I would throw open the persianas, throw off my uniform, and throw myself onto the bed. A few moments to absorb my day and my personal life would start knocking on the front door. Hello . . . hello? Judy's accusations of inadequacy, Austin's giggle, Christ's words, the gurgling of a Montana stream and the cluck cluck of parental tongues answered back. With so much judgment swirling around me, a knife, a rope and the peace of pills were my only comfort.

Suicide. I knew the answer, but was unable to find the solution that would bring me peace. Survival became a game of choices, and with a black and white mentality, I knew I could either fall into the chaos of addiction or choose the path of an Olympian. I chose the latter because I had seen my sister self-destruct, so over time I became a model military officer, tackling every shit job available and qualifying in core knowledge areas ahead of my peers. I took on every single task and became the Babe Ruth of junior officers; home run after blessed home run. The only way I existed was through herculean efforts to achieve, which masked my pain and the doubts of those around me. A superstar from sunup to sundown, as soon as I stripped my uniform off, I turned into a mime. One of those street people you see in New York City; frozen with paint on their face, and the obligatory black or white gloves. They look so lonely; you can't help but stare and wonder what caused them to want to freeze, literally, on the streets of New York. Like them, I had no current to inspire me; I lay on my bed in a frozen position, a framework of darkness and melancholy. At night, stillness caused my shadow to melt into the bed as I became a mere shadow of myself. Lost, confused and mentally unable to make sense of where I had failed myself, my marriage and most of all Christ; my personal life was torturous.

I dropped out of the military officer Bible study, was kicked out as the leader of the Youth Group on the military base and became a nomad once again. The judgment of my fellow Christians was as hot as a branding iron. They stood side by side jabbing their assumptions and judgment into me, and I stood silent for their slaughter. I was forbidden to speak my truth. If I articulated my personal dilemma, I would have been kicked out of the military. To outsiders, my marriage fell apart because of irreconcilable differences. I wanted to tell them the real difference was that I longed to feel the strength of a man between my hands, my legs, on my chest and me on his, but I couldn't. So instead, I sat in the judgment of the unknowing, allowing them to form opinions and conversation around what they observed, unable to correct them. If you were to ask my fellow military officers, they would have told you I was a good friend, and yet, they didn't know me. I carried a burden, tattooed across my chest and in my heart, hidden from sight, forcing me to conform to the Uniform Code of Military Justice, not to mention societal norms. "Why did Judy leave? What happened? Why are you getting divorced?" My answer was always the same -- a gasp of breath, a choked sob and tears that ran so fast you could hear them scream. After a while people stopped asking and I stopped talking.

I want to invite all of the talking heads who say homosexuality is a choice, a sinful choice, to choose for one day to have a relationship with a person of their same sex. A choice. I never understood that Christian proclamation, even during the height of my reparative therapy. Sexual preference is as internal to your being as your heart. It's in the center, protected behind layers of emotion, societal norms, perceptions and parental guidance. To reach in and touch it is to acknowledge life itself, and for many, that sensation is so powerful they are driven into the madness of alcoholism, drug addiction or, if you're lucky, into magnificence. Homosexuality is a gift, a precious gift, and although I couldn't unwrap this present while in a military uniform, I was comforted again that someday; a baby-blue Tiffany box would come my way. That's what kept me alive during this dark time. I believed that someday this gift would be mine. It was the same dream I held close to my heart during my days on the submarine. As a newly-divorced man, this dream came alive for me again.

What I knew for sure both in that moment and seven years prior, is that I did my very best to follow the commandment God whispered in my ear, sitting in my car in an empty parking lot in San Diego. Lucky for me, emotional intimacy was always more important than the physical connection. With Judy I had more emotional than physical satisfaction and with men my experiences were the exact opposite. Having put my trust in Christ and a reparative therapy program - my dick didn't break up the marriage, that's what I wanted to shout from the rooftops of Spain. My Johnson committed no such crime. Infidelity surrounding me like jolly ranchers in a candy store, Spain was a breeding ground for trouble amongst my heterosexual counterparts. Heterosexual men who could satisfy themselves at home stepped out to scratch their itch. I had no satisfaction and couldn't get any by stepping in or out. I was a homosexual doing the hokey pokey with no right or left foot. A gay man married to a woman, pretending to be straight to everyone – my wife included – not to mention a ruler straight life when in uniform. The only way I existed was through herculean efforts to achieve, which masked my pain and the doubt of those around me.

For those in Spain who judged my marriage, my truth is now set free. My marriage failed due to a combination of so many things: new country, new culture, long periods of separation, my inability to offer support and Judy's inability to do the same. We became a broken vessel, torn apart by a hurricane that slowly drifted out to sea — literally. A multifactorial problem, no single solution would have solved our problems. I was a military officer, put in the lockbox of a top secret clearance; I had no choice but to conform to the norm, or lose my entire career. I had already walked through the storm of one multi-year investigation, I wasn't about to go through that again and so I shut my mouth, put my head down and worked.

A few months after Judy's departure, the Commanding Officer, Navy Captain Jim Newman, offered me a promotion. A man with eyes as smart as a couture hat and as clever as a leprechaun, he remained a step ahead of every single person in our Command – which housed cryptologists working on a National Security Agency mission. I had the deepest respect for Captain Newman and held him in the highest esteem I had held any Naval Officer I had ever worked for. Trim as a flat empty envelope, he ran between six and ten miles every day at lunch, ate the same sandwich for lunch, played classical music in his office and always had the answer before he asked you a question. Getting called in to see him was eighty-five percent terror and fifteen percent pleasure, as he didn't suffer fools lightly and had no qualms about calling you a cow as he identified the bullshit that just fell from your mouth. He expected, demanded actually, one hundred percent commitment to the mission at hand. He had what I call ultimate power, just like Miranda in "The Devil Wears Prada." You could talk to him, but you better know what the fuck you're talking about and have a plan of action to either implement your solution or solutions to fix the problem. Chit chat was not his game.

When he offered me the position of Comptroller, Department Head of N8, I was stunned. He offered in the form of a question, which meant that he was telling me I would take the position and attend a three week training course in Monterey, California which started the following week. For the record, there are two kinds of promotions in the military -- rank and position. It is more common to see a person of a senior rank in a junior position which means that they are probably not going to promote in rank ever again. If, however, you see a person of junior rank in a senior position, it can be an indication that they are on a fast track, outperforming their peers. Captain Newman had just offered me the latter, and what else could I say but "Yes Sir." The next week I was on a plane to Monterey.

Smothering fog with breaths of sunlight, Monterey is a coastal town surrounded by mammoth shoreline boulders, homes and waves. It's as melancholy as a sunset painting and as inspiring as a mournful violin. I felt at home in this lonely town. Monterey has a full artillery of military personnel. To put it bluntly, this is where the military sends its smart people. Entrance into either the Defense Language Institute (DLI) or the Naval Postgraduate School (NPS) requires each student to pass a test and only a small percentage of students are admitted each year. DLI teaches over forty different languages to budding military linguists and NPS offers post-graduate education to 1,500 military officers across all services. A Lieutenant Junior Grade, I felt proud to be amongst them.

With my hotel keys secured in one pocket and my wallet in the other, my rental car led me on a chase to Big Sur. The music blaring, hair waving and sunglasses glistening, I paid extra for a convertible. With no fear of anyone knowing me, I drove with wild abandon up to Nepenthe and over to Ventana where restaurants with endless views and outdoor heaters invited me to stay all night. I spent the entire evening soaking in the words of "The Sun Also Rises" and one too many dirty martinis. Whether it was the dirty or Mr. Hemingway, Big Sur was the first place I recall feeling my spirit stir back to life.

A man indeed, I longed to feel an intimate connection. Back at the hotel I asked the concierge about a nice "night club" in Monterey. After ten minutes of nondescript answers, he finally pinned me down to "gay bar," which felt like an admission of guilt and a solution to the Rubik's cube all in the same breath. I didn't want sex; I wanted to connect with men. I wanted to laugh, stare, talk and feel their breath hit my face, like God's whisper in my ear. In the company of men all day long, it's different when you walk into a gay bar. The guys at work were like brothers to me. I couldn't look into their eyes with unabashed pleasure or glance down to check out their packages; it would have felt like incest. I trusted the men at work to have my back in a time of need, and they trusted me to navigate turbulent times. We shared a brotherly bond, and sex was just never part of the equation. Sexual energy is similar to jamming a radar signal. It confuses both the sender and the receiver, and I was famous for keeping the lines of communication clear –– crystal clear. The men who worked for me had no misconceptions about who was in charge or what I expected from them.

Gay bars, however, are radar-jamming central. It's like stepping into the closet of a Chronicles of Narnia book. Men look at men, women look at women, and you can get chatted up, chatted about or chattered over all in a matter of minutes. One eye towards the door at all times, gay men are consummate multitaskers. They can look at you, flirt with the bartender, watch the back door and keep an eye on the bathroom while standing outside smoking a cigarette tying their shoes. Hyper vigilance is taught at a very young age; suspecting parents, classmates, friends or girlfriends –– gay men have to know what you are feeling or thinking before you tell them. It's the only way they can survive.

When I walked into the bar I felt all eyes on me and it was all I could do to not turn around and walk out. I hadn't been in a gay bar as an openly gay man in over eight years. I quickly scanned the room and then made my way to the dark end of the bar, grabbed a beer, and slunk over to the side of the darkest wall to watch. Funny thing about me is that I am the life of a party in a heterosexual bar and a bar napkin in a gay bar. I will sing Karaoke, take my shirt off, dance, down shot after shot, get a little too wild and crazy with the ladies while I discreetly check out their boyfriends at a straight bar, but a gay bar leaves me all wet like the rivulets of sweat pouring down a bottle of Bud Light. Talk to a hot guy in a gay bar? I would rather crawl under the table than approach a hot guy. That fateful night I was like a newborn calf, my spirit still weak from the traumatic birth of my pending divorce, I did a lot of staring, and not a lot of talking. Until I met Keith.

Like a jet-black car in the dead of night, he blindsided me before I had a chance to crash under the bar and hide. Six foot something, deep brown eyes, jet-black hair, a brown and black goatee, and an Italian nose, I don't remember the first ten things he said to me. It wasn't until he told me to relax, he wasn't going to attack me that I actually laughed. He looked like a Chow Chow with squinty eyes and tamed-down hair. You know those dogs, the ones you want to cuddle like a stuffed animal? That was Keith. Before I knew it he had his chocolate in my peanut butter. I'm not sure how long we talked, but the evening wound its way to his friend Aleah's house where we had more cocktails and then a few more. Taking a play out of my mother's nun playbook, I politely left at an unreasonable hour, with a firm handshake and a promise to stay in touch. It really was as innocent as that. Not a kiss goodbye or a pinch on his chubby Chow Chow cheeks. I swear!

My days in Monterey rolled in and out like the waves outside my window, and before I knew it I had aced the test and graduated as the youngest member of the class. School had always been easy for me. I was the one guy who paid attention to the teacher and took good notes so I didn't have to pay the piper later. My free time was too valuable to me, so when in uniform, I was focused like a laser beam. I don't think Keith ever saw me in uniform. Every night after class I would change out of my uniform and then head over to his house for a dinner or some drinks. He gave me what I needed; good conversation that was matched with some good eats and wine. I know, I know, I know . . . there comes a point when talking can ruin the prospect of anything sexual because you get to know the person, maybe a little too well, right? Sometimes it's more fun to fornicate without confabulating, but we never forayed into the forbidden forest. Instead, we talked, and talked, and talked. My feelings bordered between curiosity and the satisfaction of having made a new friend. I spent quite a bit of time with Keith during the three week stay, and I headed back to Spain unsure of whether I wanted to frolic or have a friend in him. Keith insisted he drive me to the airport, so with my rental car returned, he pulled me curbside with a repeated invitation to join him in Saint Felix, France the following month, a vacation he had long since planned. My new job ahead of me, I knew that now was not the time for a foray into France.

Back in Spain, the nights were as lonely and barren as the streets of New York at 4 a.m. I was a one-armed paperhanger at work, learning the ropes of my new job, and at night I would stay late so I could email Keith on the unclassified computer. The whirring of the air conditioner and my mind, that's what kept me company in the stillness of my work cave as everyone said their goodbyes for the day and shut down their offices. Alone at last, I became the man I was in Monterey-- nervous, excited, anxious and full of hope. Email after email, with my workday done and Keith's workday just beginning, I'm not sure how he got anything accomplished.

Keith kept asking me about France, and while I wasn't ready to say no, I also hadn't been completely honest with him. I had a disease I hadn't told him about, a disease that worsened with each military assignment and promotion. I was struck with the disease known as workaholism, and I knew the French were intolerant about stamping the passports of those of us infected. I didn't know how to relax, and the thought of clearing French customs with nothing but time waiting on the other side terrified me so I stalled, hemmed and hawed.

A quick trip to Bahrain for a week, where the airlines lost my luggage on the way there and back, allowed me some breathing room to put Keith off. I was asked to re-enlist one of my favorite sailors, Kathy Keefe. A sailor's sailor, she had the courage of a lion and the determination of a warrior. It was my honor to re-enlist her back into the Navy for several more years, one of the most cherished requests a sailor can ask of a Naval Officer.

It's a sign of respect, and for Kathy, it went both ways. With the ceremony completed, I headed back to Spain and decided to take a risk.

Three weeks later I landed in Paris. A chance to shed my military skin and live as a man, who happens to be gay, sounded like freedom and terror wrapped into one. As I got off the plane in France I remember mumbling down the jet way that I had walked away from the gay lifestyle to get married, and was now getting a divorce, how much harder could this trip be? Nervous as an alley cat, I found Keith waiting for me, smiling like he had just eaten the canary. I still have the photo that a tourist took of Keith and me in the Paris airport. Distant arms around each other, smiling like brothers, nothing touching but our shoulders, we definitely looked like we were hiding a secret. Keith looked like a Roman guard with a goatee and I looked like an uncomfortable accountant. On film, there was no way I could deny my presence or the journey I was about to take.

Saint Felix, France. With a population of 1,301 people and 130,000 sunflowers, the beauty burst from the landscape like a Monet painting. Winding roads, wildflowers, and a deep blue sky, I could not deny the beauty of southern France. Situated on a hilltop with the Pyrenees as a backdrop, this town was home to monasteries and a hermitage — my mother would have been so proud. Without as much as an orange or a breadstick, we made our way to the store before heading back to the chateau.

Chateau — that word just sounds sexy, doesn't it? We were greeted with an ensconced home, hidden amongst the trees, set back from the road, with windows that peered above the treetops. Big hulking stones held the house together, which was adorned by yellow wood shutters outlined in black trim that winked at you in the morning, and at night. A ten-foot dark- stained wood front door beckoned us inside while the lion's mouth knocker sat on the door watching our every move. With no expectation of arriving guests, we had the six bedrooms, three bathrooms, and a bottom floor kitchen all to ourselves — a terrifying thought really. We made our way inside to ignite the pilot light, fling open the wooden shutters and shake out the dust. Romantic and awkward, there we stood in the family chateau of one of Keith's best friends, the silence speaking for us.

The "us" part is what made me squirm. For the past seven years, "us" meant Jesus Christ, Judy and more recently, Austin. Keith's definition of "us" was his gaggle of male friends, family and his life in Monterey. On the verge of opening up a furniture store, France had called him away from his California life to de-stress and put some distance between him and a crazy stalker in San Francisco, which I found out after we arrived. Make no mistake, the crazy stalker found him in France, called the house repeatedly and cancelled Keith's return plane ticket to America. Unaccustomed to this type of drama, and unsure of Keith's expectations, I felt like a scientist trying to piece together the DNA of a genome project.

The nights found us turning on the external spotlights, taking scary pictures of our faces, rolling on the lawn in laughter, and creating formidable hand puppet shows on the outside house walls. A block of cheese in one hand and a sturdy handful of French bread in the other, we took turns answering the phone in our best French accents as the stalker put us on speed redial. We took long walks amongst sunflowers that danced above our heads, lost in a maze of yellow and emotion. The days found us in the kitchen; bodies pressed together, with tumbled words dried on the floor along with my tears. He never reached out to dry my eyes; he just let me cry tears of confusion. I would have rather shown my ass in the local town square than break down and cry in the arms of a man I barely knew, but there I was, doing both.

Romance found us wrapped arm in arm, cuddled under a down blanket with the breeze of France blowing in. His hairy chest pressed against my back, or my smooth chest pressed against his hairy back. A man who loves nothing more than to sleep the way I came out of my mother's womb, I kept my underwear firmly in place. I know what Keith wanted, but he was too polite to pressure me. We burrowed, spooned, bundled, huddled, nestled and snuggled. My seven-year dream of feeling the strength of a man between my hands, my legs, on my chest and me on his finally came true. I felt alive and broken, knowing that this was what I wanted for my future but unsure of how to get there. I wasn't sure I wanted to get back into the rat race, but I knew I wanted to win a prize worthy of my intentions. Keith showed me the roadmap without taking me to the end point, and I was grateful for his lead.

As we scurried around the chateau, the phone silenced, the cheese eaten and the wine bottles deposited outside, I could feel heaviness in the air. The possibility of a relationship was 5,926 miles apart and my heart was even further. I was unable to give myself to anything but my work and was unsure of a future with a man, any man. I lugged our luggage downstairs and with six hours to arrive at the airport, I heard Keith turn on the water upstairs. Long, slow, steady drips of water, I put my book down and walked upstairs to check in. Keith was sitting in a white clawfoot bathtub that rested in the corner, beneath a winking window. Our eyes locked and he turned his head, inviting me to join him. Birds chirping, sunflowers smiling and the wind whispering our fate, we sat together in silence, my muscular legs and his beefy chest entwined in the daylight. Two men attempting to fit the puzzle pieces of our sadness together, we departed with more despair than the hope of our hello. My heart bursting from a new experience and the loneliness waiting for me in Spain, I returned back to my marble floor apartment, military career and my trustworthy 1978 push-button start Ford Fiesta.

PACO

(Ages 31 -32)

It was after my trip to France that the mirror looked back at me and smiled when it told me I was gay. No longer a sneer, I was able to smile back and trust the reflection's wish that my future would indeed hold a ray of hope. Hope came on a hot October evening when I ran, literally, right into Paco. Head down, music blaring and the sun dipping below the horizon, I was running without paying attention. Paco came up on me, a six foot plus hunk of a man careening on the beach, traveling on his own journey. Fate reached out and pressed us together. A muscly sinew of a tree trunk, he had on blue shorts, a bright red shirt with yellow trim along the neck and a big silver watch on his right arm. I tripped and stumbled a bit, he laughed, and then we said hello. If I had known what awaited me, I would have said goodbye in that same moment, but my desire to be with a man that I could love was so strong, that I said hello again for the next two years.

Paco invited himself and a friend over to my apartment the same day I met him and I ran out to get bread, wine and cheese. He brought his bright blue Audi TT, which he parked right in front of my building. Unsure of his intentions, or mine, I had convinced myself that he and his buddy found Americans fascinating and were coming over to hang out. I, however, was wondering how he was hung as my libido hadn't fired up to this decibel level since I was a nineteen-year-old kid. Yeah, I was unapologetically horny. I had just lost my son, my wife, my dreams, my faith in Christ, was working 14+ hour days, living in a foreign country where my every move was monitored by a security clearance that was tied around my neck like a boulder — oh fuck yeah I was hoping to get laid. France had left me unmistakably famished, and I wasn't about to pass up a possible feast for the second time.

Fresh off the boulevard of broken dreams, Paco rolled out the red carpet of hope and inspiration. A shop owner, masculine, shy, and with a reserved nature, I could be seen out in town with him and not raise as much as one military eyebrow of suspicion. Paco lived in Jerez de la Frontera, a town thirty minutes from mine, which my 1978 Ford Fiesta made once and then died along-side of the road. It was the only thing that died between Paco and I as he continued to drive down to spend evenings and weekends with me. We toured Spain and Portugal like Thelma and Louise minus the convertible. Our cultural differences caused heated discussions and even more heat in the bedroom, which was the glue that held us together for the first few months. It was an unabashed fuck fest –- exactly what I needed.

A few months into our relationship, just as we started talking about moving in together Paco tripped on the sidewalk and dropped some pills on the ground. Vitamins, that's what he said. Bullshit, that's what I said. It took me forty-five minutes to pull the truth out of him. Through jagged tears, Paco broke down and told me of his HIV status. I was on the verge of telling him that I loved him when this newsflash sped across the newsreel of my life. We had been together for several passion-filled months and he hadn't said a word. He sobbed as he sat on his couch, the truth exposing him, and me. I did the only thing I could think of in that moment. I picked up his car keys, packed up my clothes and walked out the door.

HIV positive? My thoughts spun to Chuck as I drove back to the base. Chuck was killed by a secret and I was walking a fine line between my secret life at night and the secrets I kept at work. Possible HIV exposure had just put my job and my life on the line. I was required to take an annual physical exam where I was routinely tested for the HIV virus. If I had contracted it, I would lose my job and my clearance, and be sent back to the United States, ending my career as a Naval Officer. As an HIV positive service member, I could no longer be assigned to Navy ships or overseas or take any assignment outside of the immediate vicinity of a Naval Hospital.

I didn't talk to Paco for several weeks. I kept his car on the base where he couldn't enter and retrieve it, a form of payback for the pain he had just caused me. I booked a plane ticket to Montana, dropped Paco's car off at the airport and went home to see Austin and my family.

I spent the holidays in turmoil. Break up with Paco? Stay together? I had no answers. I felt love for Paco and believed that I was in love with him, but the clock was ticking on my tour in Spain and within less than two years I would be returning back to America for a new assignment. Should I stay with Paco and risk my health, or should I break it off and spend the rest of my time in solitude? I couldn't stand the thought of going drinking with my military buddies, pretending to check out tits and ass night after night. Going to dinner with couples who talked about their kids was beyond my ability. I was now in a desk job with no hope for travel, so I couldn't accept a temporary assignment in Italy or Greece. So this is what HIV looked like . . . a massive ball of confusion.

Returning to Spain on the heartbreak of seeing Austin and the comforts of home, I couldn't face being alone. Risking everything I had worked for, I returned to Paco. The only thing stable in my life besides work, Paco's hug felt like a warm Jacuzzi after a cold shower of emotional uncertainty. We laid out new ground rules, I laid out a fresh batch of condoms, and he promised truth in every aspect of his life. I had put my trust in God so many years before when I turned my life over to Christ and walked away from the homosexual lifestyle to get married; this was another leap of faith -- just in the opposite direction.

I kept my apartment in Rota, just in case, but moved in with Paco shortly after my return from Montana. He introduced me to his family, his business associate, and I in turn introduced him to my fellow military officers. A friend, that's what I said he was. They couldn't ask more and I couldn't say anything else; my life teetered between fact and fiction. Dinner parties, elaborate four course meals that his mother whipped up and late night dinners with his sisters, I lived as if I were never going to leave Spain.

I completed a master's degree and with six months before my departure, I received my military orders. I had been accepted to the Naval Postgraduate School in Monterey to obtain a second master's degree in Financial Management. I was told it would hurt my career as I wasn't headed to a ship and back out to sea, but I didn't care. Education is the one thing that could never be taken away from me, and if the Navy was willing to send me to school, I wasn't going to pass it up.

My final three months tasted like the last bite of a delicious meal. Paco and I spent every moment possible together, soaking it all in. He was unable to move to America due to his HIV status and I had a child to support and an ex-wife asking for the one thing she said she never would — a piece of my retirement. With obligations tied around my ankles, there was no getting out of my departure. It lurched, heaved, twisted and shouted at me as I made my way through my final few months. At a farewell party from my fellow military officers, Paco came along and I toasted my brothers and sisters in uniform, and boldly thanked Paco for his friendship.

Unable to say goodbye, Paco closed up his store in Spain and bought a plane ticket to Montana, where he arrived three days after I had touched down. We had one month to spend together before I was scheduled to check into the Naval Postgraduate School and begin my next assignment. For one blissful month we roamed the mountains of Montana, drove down to Vegas to press our luck, over to Palm Springs to warm the air outside of the bedroom and up to Monterey where Paco got on the plane back to Spain and I got an anonymous HIV test at a local health clinic to confirm I was still negative. Chris and Amy A. from Spain had also received orders to Monterey so I was not completely alone.

As I drove Paco to the airport in my brand new BMW convertible, we vowed to stay in touch and travel to see one another once every three months, but I knew my workaholic twin would not allow that. Once I sunk my teeth into the academic rigor that awaited me, I knew I wouldn't leave until I had my diploma in hand. I openly gave Paco a full kiss on the lips in the San Francisco airport. Gay and determined not to let my military rank suffocate my personal life anymore, I was saying goodbye to the first man I ever truly loved. Paco. I never saw him again.

MONTEREY, CA
(Ages 32 -33)

Focused squarely on my schoolwork, I began the dance of all work and no play. With Paco back in Spain, and my heart along with him, I made no room for anything other than my schoolbooks. I rekindled a friendship with Keith but steered clear of developing a group of gay friends. Monterey is smaller than Missoula and there was no way I was going to risk my career by being an openly gay man in a town this small. I was slated to complete a second master's degree, a master of science in Financial Management, and write a several-hundred page thesis all within a two year period. Surrounded by military officers, both men and women from all branches of the services, attending the Naval Postgraduate School was an honor and one I did not take lightly.

I stayed in the closet and out of the light for the first six months. Calculus, statistics, accounting, business management, economics, and a myriad of other courses, I had no time to hit the golf course or veer off course. San Francisco was a two-hour drive and by the time Friday night rolled around the last thing I wanted to do was roll my car up the California freeway to stand and look at men in a bar. Instead, I bought a piano and took lessons, a lifelong dream I let slip through my fingers at age nine and I was determined to play again.

I became a café junkie, a man who hated coffee but hung out at all of the local cafes with my books in one hand and my computer in the other. My apartment in Marina was about a twenty-five minute drive, the last apartment complex before the sand dunes took over the landscape until the next town appeared thirty miles away. With my recent divorce and my junior rank, this apartment was all I could afford and it was all I could do to force myself to go home to the loneliness awaiting me.

Home is exactly what Dan was trying to avoid. Dan. The man I met at a local café one Sunday afternoon. I had seen him there before, but really didn't pay that much attention for I was buried in my schoolwork. This day, however, was different. We struck up a conversation about the city, my studies and his work. I glanced down and noticed the wedding ring on his finger, but before long I realized our conversation was working its way toward the subtle dance that homosexuals perform. I had no intention of sleeping with Dan, for my heart was 5,000 miles away and Dan had a wife and two kids at home. I could see the pain in Dan's eyes as we sat across from each other, a pain that had lingered in my own eyes for the seven years I was married. I understood this man almost better than he understood himself and for the first time in my life I reached out to another human being with the tenderness of understanding; a man trapped in a marriage unsure of how to get out.

Don't you wonder what it must feel like to be trapped in a cage with no escape? Most men who have homosexual desires and get married never openly acknowledge that they are gay, and some have no idea. Yet, as time moves forward, life gets shorter and self-awareness grows and it becomes an impossible task to ignore sexuality conflicts. For those men who have built a family with a woman and have no desire to lead an openly gay life, the prospect of "coming out" to the family is horrifyingly frightening. Dan was the first man I had ever met whose circumstances paralleled my own. Married for 20+ years, he knew he needed to acknowledge his truth but didn't know how.

With a blossoming friendship that was constantly teetering on the edge of intimacy, Dan broke the news to his wife after we broke bread at a local restaurant. I had been giving Dan the best advice I could, and as he pulled away from the parking lot I sat down and prayed for him — the first prayers I had said in several years. I knew his pain, understood his dilemma, and I also knew that someday the conflict would manifest itself in ways that neither of us could fully comprehend. I have to say that I've never met a more honorable man. Dan faced his truth before he stepped out on his wife and spoke the words "I'm gay" aloud to her, allowing her the opportunity to pick up the pieces of their marriage with dignity.

I'm not sure how it feels to be a woman and receive the news that your husband of 20+ years is gay. I suppose it's akin to a diagnosis of terminal cancer or something just as shocking. What was understood and accepted as a partnership in marriage is suddenly shattered by the news that one of you has been leading an inauthentic life. I guess it's true about what they say; half the truth is a whole lie. I felt hollow inside as I thought about the pain and turmoil they were dealing with. My heart went out to her as I truly don't believe she had any idea of Dan's secret. With his secret revealed, it took several months for him to feel any sense of relief. Liberated on one hand and bound by the guilt of having just torn a family apart, there was no winner in this situation.

Dan and I maintained a friendship throughout the remainder of my tour in Monterey. Serious and quiet, he caused me to reflect on my own life's circumstances while I challenged him with esoteric thinking and laughter. I believed that if the circumstances of our lives had been different, there may have been room for a relationship, but I still had several more years of military life ahead of me and I was bound and determined to retire with a full pension.

Towards the end of my tour in Monterey and with my thesis in Appreciative Inquiry complete, I relit my passion to sing and joined a local theater company for two stage productions. A theatrical performance in front of anyone but my comb and Mariah Carey had always made me squirm with embarrassment. Yet, there I was up on the "Western Stage" singing and dancing with a cast of musical daredevils. Sarah Jebian was my inspiration, my vocal coach, and the woman with whom I developed a "stage crush." She dared me to sing louder, dance brighter and let my inner "diva" fly out of my body up on that stage. A magical moment in time for me, I was finally able to leave my uniform at home when I walked out the door and into the civilian life of the theater.

Nearing the end of my tour in Monterey, Vice Admiral Harms, who was the Chief of Naval Education, called me into a conference room one afternoon and asked me to come and work with him to further my thesis work. He told me that while it may hurt my career in the short term, he would do everything in his power to secure a competitive job for me when my assignment was complete. Since it's impossible to say no to a three star Admiral, I accepted the position and began traveling around the country with professors from Case Western University, the Naval Postgraduate School and Vice Admiral Harms. The assignment lasted close to a year and by the time it was over Vice Admiral Harms had made good on his promise.

I was assigned to a one-year remote tour in Saudi Arabia with Joint Task Force South West Asia where I would serve as the only Naval Cryptologic Officer with the United States Air Force.

KINGDOM OF SAUDI ARABIA

(Age 34 - 35)

With five years and one month remaining towards my goal of completing a twenty-year career in the military, I needed to remain professionally competitive amongst my military peers. While education is revered, and I had just completed my second master's degree, the majority of my contemporaries were busy taking tough assignments on ships and in places that allowed them to expand their knowledge of cryptology. Spain was my first tour as a cryptologic officer and the Naval Postgraduate School was my second. I knew that if I wanted to stay competitive and promote up the ranks, a remote assignment in Saudi Arabia was my only option.

President Bush was busy beating his war drum as I drove my little BMW Z3 convertible from Monterey up the coast of Oregon and over to Montana in November of 2002. I was the only driver on the road with California plates, the top town, a hat and earmuffs as snow fell from the sky. I drove with the music cranked up as loud as it would go, my nose turning as bright red as Rudolph's. I knew the next year would be a lonely assignment so I drove with wild abandon, stopping to see friends and Austin along my way back home to Montana.

While I had found peace through my divorce, my time in Monterey was a stark reminder that leading a gay life can be lonely. I couldn't live an openly gay life; I was too scared to date a man for fear that if it ended badly he would turn me in to the military authorities and with a top secret clearance, I knew the rules of not asking and not telling anyone about my newfound freedom. Free at last, I felt constrained in my new skin. Paco was forbidden to move to America, one night stands in San Francisco repulsed me and I knew I couldn't get serious about someone because I was forced to move every few years. I was stuck between dating a man who didn't have a serious job -- the type I usually wasn't attracted to -- and dating a man with a serious career who couldn't sacrifice his for mine. I was a man in my mid-thirties who wasn't available to anyone I'd give a second look. Saudi Arabia. I had nothing to lose.

Before I left for Saudi Arabia, I received a set of follow-on orders to the headquarters of the National Security Agency in Fort Meade, Maryland. Having never been to Maryland I was excited by the prospect of living in either Baltimore or Washington, DC after my yearlong tour was complete in the Kingdom. I knew I would spend the next twelve months in isolation, serving alongside the Air Force in a country and within an infrastructure that were completely foreign to me. I had never served near the front lines of anything, and it was painfully obvious to me that President Bush wasn't going to back down. I was headed towards the action for the next twelve months.

As I readied myself to go, I wondered what kind of compromises I would have to make with regards to my sexuality. Would my status as a single male draw the attention of single females? Deployments can be very lonely, and it's not uncommon for romances to develop and quite possibly, sexual encounters. I didn't want to have to explain myself or turn away any interested parties so I chose the safest route possible. I bought myself a wedding ring and placed it on my left hand, hoping to avoid all questions regarding my family life. For all intents and purposes, I was a Naval Officer who was married with a child. That was my story, and I was sticking to it.

My paternal grandmother, Harriett, a saint of woman who never had a bad word to say about anyone, baked me a cake the night before I left for Saudi Arabia. As I stood in her kitchen with my family gathered around, I wondered if this was the last time she would see me, or I would see her. Quiet and reserved, I could see the pride in my grandmother's eyes as she looked at one of her first grandchildren to finish college and the first to obtain a master's degree. She took my hand in hers and rubbed it back and forth, quietly uttering her prayers for safety and a safe return. As I boarded the plane to fly to Maryland where my plane to the Kingdom of Saudi Arabia was waiting, it was the first time I ever cried while leaving home.

There's something magical about packing up your life, tucking it all away in a storage shed, gathering your life's possessions in a couple of suitcases and embarking on a journey to unknown lands. I had been doing this since the tender age of sixteen and now, twice that age, I was headed towards an unknown adventure with fear in my heart and a song of hope in my head. As I landed at the Baltimore Washington International Airport, I had a one-day delay before my plane left for Saudi. I met a fellow military officer, Karim, with whom I had formed a friendship in Bahrain several years prior. He picked me up and took me around Baltimore as I slowly began to think about where I wanted to live once I returned from the Kingdom. Karim convinced me that Baltimore was a better choice and a shorter commute to the National Security Agency than DC would be and so with that I met a realtor that same day, gave him a check for $25,000 and told him I wanted a two bedroom two bathroom condo with a view of the city. Unsure if I would live or die in Saudi Arabia, the only thing I knew for sure was that I would own a condo in downtown Baltimore.

As I stepped off the plane in Saudi Arabia I braced myself for the oven like heat and was instead greeted by a torrential downpour of rain, complete with thunder and lightning. I was pulling two pieces of luggage and my briefcase, none of which had Goodyear tires to ground me. There were about 200 military personnel on the plane, but there were only two of us who were considered "permanent party" – assigned to Saudi Arabia for one year – so I got to move to the front of the line. True to form, the security detail ripped my luggage apart looking for any prohibited items to include pictures of women with skin showing – laughable -- I know.

Days quickly turned to weeks which morphed into one month and then two, and then a full scale war on March 19th, 2003. I remember that date because I was standing in my workspace waiting for CNN to pick up the story on the bombing and I was surprised at how long it took them to broadcast this news. A singular marker of time within the three months I had been in Saudi Arabia, I had met a lot of people but yet I knew no-one. We didn't stand around and talk about family, our kids or our parents. We talked about work. Every single conversation was focused on work, what the next event was, how the past tied into the present and the crisis of the moment. I was a man surrounded by hundreds of people living in complete solitude.

This abrupt change was a welcome reprieve from my life in America; the loneliness, divorce, feelings of failure in the eyes of Christ and my wife – yes – I loved the busy solitude in the beginning. Once the war started and our team settled into a daily cadence, the routine of my life began to wear me down like a saggy old mattress. I felt myself bend in the middle from the weight on my shoulders and I was no longer satisfied in the business of military events.

I began to conjure up the taboo memories of my past like a young kid playing with an Ouija board. It was foolish to even think I could entertain a sexual encounter on a military base in the middle of Saudi Arabia, but my hormones were cheering me on from the sidelines. Pilots, Navigators, Intel Officers and hundreds of other military men surrounded me, ten percent of which I believed were also homosexual, but the question was how was I supposed to identify the ten percent? I couldn't ask, they couldn't tell and I sucked at the double meaning game while in uniform. My computer was monitored, pay per view was forbidden and I lived in a cement cell with walls so thick that nobody could hear my hormones no matter how loud they screamed.

While I wasn't in a unique situation with regards to my sexual frustration, it would have been nice to have a gay friend to talk with. I have no doubt that every single man around me was angling for a piece of action, which the military made clear was off limits. Sex between consenting adults while stationed overseas was strictly prohibited and I knew the military authorities meant business. Husbands and wives weren't even allowed to bunk together – the military required them to live in separate facilities with members of the same sex. For those that were on a 90 day assignment this rule seemed doable, but for a guy like me who was on a 360 day assignment, I wasn't sure which head would explode first.

At the end of April my solitary sleeping quarters were taken away from me as the Saudi Arabian government ordered us to leave their country within twenty-four hours. The General had warned us one day prior to the official announcement, and with no idea of where I was going to live, I was told that I would be shipped to Doha, Qatar to live in a tent in Camp Andy. With the exception of one suitcase, every personal belonging I owned was shipped back to the United States.

Qatar was quite a change from my life in Saudi Arabia as there weren't any buildings or facilities other than what the Air Force created using tents. Camp Andy wasn't prepared to receive hundreds of soldiers on a twenty-four hour notice, and the transition felt like an unorganized ant hill. I was lucky enough to land a cot in a twelve man tent located 1.5 miles from work and 0.5 miles from the bathroom. I quickly learned the trick of peeing in a bottle and drinking all of the water available to me as I traipsed through the dusty sand twice a day in 110+ degree heat.

The one accommodation the Air Force ensured was in place upon our arrival was their Security Force Team. They were assigned to drive around in Humvees late at night with heat-seeking cameras to catch those who thought they could break the rule of no copulation while confined in a foreign country. The stories we heard about people confabulating on top of water towers, behind soldier's tents and in parked cars made all of us roar with laughter. The threat of being caught by the infamous heat seeking camera was enough to keep my Johnson tucked away for the remainder of my tour.

In June of 2003 I was given my first "rest and relaxation" trip back to the United States. It was my first break after six months of steady work. Thrilled beyond words, I had made plans to fly home to Montana and pick up Austin, who was in Kindergarten. When I landed back in America I called Judy, who sharply informed me that Austin couldn't afford to miss one day of Kindergarten and that I would have to cancel the plane tickets I had purchased to California and my two tickets to Disneyland. Dumbfounded, I hung up the phone.

Judy's rationalization that Austin could not miss one day of Kindergarten when I had not seen him in close to seven months left me speechless. She was becoming increasingly resistant to the custody agreement outlined in our divorce decree, and this was her first overt gesture towards me. I had been operating from a premise of guilt, buying her a new computer before I left for Saudi, new snow tires for her car, giving her our joint owned timeshare and on and on and on. Of course I felt guilty about our divorce, as I married her with the purest of intentions – but she was now making me pay by taking time away with my son. I returned home to Montana, went and got Austin and spent the remainder of my vacation with him – at my parent's house.

Back in Qatar with six months remaining on my tour, I spent my days sleeping and my nights working. My lunch breaks took place at around 4am where I would put on my running gear and head out the door to a cool breeze and twinkly sky. I routinely watched the fighter jets take off with their after burners going full blast. They looked like fireflies speeding off into the night. Some nights I positioned myself at the end of the runway tempting the wind and fuel to carry me to America, back home

Although I kept a journal my entire year in Saudi Arabia and Qatar, the only entry that feels right to share is the final one I wrote before I headed back to the United States to settle down in Maryland. I think this journal entry captures my feeling of professional accomplishment, and the mental anguish of serving in a remote military tour for 360 days:

Journal Entry November 2003 – Last Transmission – Doha Qatar

I am gone. As your eyes dance across the bits and bytes that have been re-assembled on the screen before you, I am defying life in a different way – I am flying across the world to my new home.

I know I'm not breaking the sound barrier, but I have decoded an unspoken barrier between the generation of my parents and the generation serving in Iraq and Afghanistan. It's the barrier of combat. I used to associate that word with stories and movies about Vietnam, a part of my parent's history I never quite understood. Now, as I stand in the heat of the desert or the cool mountains of Afghanistan I know that my legs spread over a pace in time that they'll never quite understand. How did time slip by so quickly that I now have the answers to the questions my parents will never know to ask? I fear, I have become a man.

Chuck was a man amongst men. I still wonder what it was like for Chuck to sit on the edge of his bed with the gun pointed at his head. I wonder if he was crying, what he was mumbling, if he felt calm and how he consciously accepted death in that moment. His departure was not an accident like drowning, where you have no control over it. He was in full control; at least of the trigger, and knowing Chuck, probably very conscientious of the clean-up that occurred afterward.

I first met Chuck in 1987, over 15 years ago. I walked into a bar and there he was with his cowboy boots, cowboy hat and stupid grin. I didn't like him at first as he was overbearing, always wanting to make a deal and very opinionated. He reminded me of that Monty Hall guy on "Let's Make a Deal." Fast talker, pushy and never really focused on the moment; that was Chuck.....I miss him.

He is a connection in my life that I still long to have. It's been a bit like dialing a phone number only to find out that your friend has moved. That, however, hasn't stopped me from talking to him as he was the first person I ever met from the Air Force. Little did I know that 15 years later I would be serving with a contingency of them in the middle of the desert for one straight year?

I haven't ever mentioned Chuck in any of my journal entries home, as Chuck was a private person and I know he wouldn't want me talking about him – especially behind his back. It is now time to close the door on this connection I have kept alive. Chuck, an Air Force Sergeant. A shotgun blast. A good friend. A body ravaged by AIDS. A desert companion. A sacrificed life – I wonder how many lessons he left behind?

I no longer want to hear "the lessons" the pundits on television state that we are learning or need to learn about the low-grade conflicts in Iraq and Afghanistan. Fuck them. Yes, harsh words for a harsh reality that is so misunderstood I no longer know where to begin my story so that you can follow along and understand it with me. The questions, speculation, and constant drone of talking heads make me thankful that we've invented newspapers that recycle themselves and electronic media that can be turned off with a single click. The truth is that there is no definitive truth – it is a situation evolving – much like a human being. What appeared to be absolute at 16 years old looks absurd at 26 and so on. Iraq. Afghanistan. We've only just begun.

The truth is that it is exactly six paces and twelve paces from the door of my tent to the edge of my bed. You might think that it is impossible to be both, but it isn't. I know, because I have counted them in the dark for the last 184 days.

When I have my boots on I count six paces in the dark and I can reach out and touch my bed. When I have my running shoes on I count twelve paces in the dark and I can reach out and touch my bed. How did I discover this? That's like asking me when I discovered I could speak Spanish. One day I just woke up and it poured from my mouth like chocolate syrup on vanilla ice cream.

Six paces, twelve paces, six paces, twelve paces….why? If how I behave is directly related to what I put on my feet, how in good conscious can I ignore the influences of my environment? When my mom had her high heels on she probably slinked across a fancy restaurant in twenty saunters, but in her tennis shoes I bet she marched right to the bathroom like a woman with a mission in nine sharp salutes.

I wonder how your behavior would change if you were forced to carry a gun and wear a flak jacket? Think about that the next time you defend the argument that environment does not affect our behavior.

Biologically wired…..environmentally influenced. Did God do me any favors when I said "I do?" Shoes…who would have thought?

I used to think I understood convolution. My feet have skimmed across four different continents for the past 19 years and swam underneath the ocean for two of those. The only thing I know for sure is that it really is harder than it looks on paper.

The best paper I saw all year came in two forms; a white envelope with my Grandma Harriet's handwriting on it and a white box with a weekly delivery of banana bread from my friend Dan. They served as reminders that life outside of the desert was progressing and evolving. Thank you.

You are being fed a line of bullshit. Have you ever seen a person lie? They tend to blink or blush or look away. Now, they sit and stare into a screen and read the words that play across it. They aren't looking at you, they are reading sentences put together by organizations that think they know what you need to hear and believe in order to keep the economy afloat and our society from ripping apart at the seams. When will you reach your limit? Are you really just too comfortable in your recliner or shopping at the local Wal-Mart, Staples, Home Depot, Lowes, or Old Navy stores to give a shit? What price is your complacency causing you? Jingle bells….jingle bells…..it's time to let the music lull you, the TV transfix you, the shopping malls overwhelm you – all in the name of - ???? Life is happening – what does your life stand for?

I remember the day Austin stood up for the first time. His facial expression communicated a thought of "how did I get up here?", and of course, he grinned – not really sure what he was grinning about. A teenager with spiked hair, a young adult graduating from college, a thirty year old standing at the altar, a forty year old buying a new corvette, a fifty year old looking at a retirement account, a sixty year old standing at the grave of his parents, a seventy year old attending a second wedding of their first born child, an eighty year old mastering arthritis with grace, a ninety year old reflecting on memories…. It comes in increments of ten for a reason. How fortunate am I to have lived two years in the time-span of one.

One day a few weeks ago I was walking back from the bathroom and stumbled upon an anthill. There were about thirty ants digging tunnels into and beneath the sand. I kicked dirt over them, into their holes and then stepped down; just to make sure I sent a clear message. I then sat down in the sand and stared at my accomplishment. Ten minutes passed and nothing happened. My curiosity took over and I dug at the ground. Within minutes the scouts came barging up out of the ground scouring for evidence as if someone had committed a crime. Then the workers made their way forward and began digging again, just as if nothing had happened. Within 45 minutes they re-established their working positions and were busy digging tunnels once again.

I wonder at what point our memories get erased. When do we decide that the threat is over and it's time to move forward again? What's the price we pay for forgetting? My foot, which had crushed them less than an hour before was standing by to wreak havoc again – but they were oblivious to it. I wonder….what are you oblivious to?

Secrets – there's only one secret keeper that is receiving my farewell message. Air Force Captain Kim Noble. You are deserving of a paragraph if not a page. I rarely stand up to applaud a good performance, but for you – I would sing from the balconies. My deepest bow and most humble gratitude – thank you for keeping me afloat this past year. I will miss you Shipmate.

And so it goes - my most coined phrase "Shipmate" will finally cease to be spoken, at least for my ears. I suppose my legacy here will be more than a word or a thought – but that's not for me to decide. Instead, I go forward with my head held high and a full feeling in my heart. I arrived believing that I understood variance, a graduate with two master's degrees. I leave knowing that there is no way to define life's standard deviations from the mean. It is bloody if not unpredictable, and theories belong in textbooks, not as outcomes that are spewed forth from television screens or preachers.

Outcomes are created through diversity and challenge. Yet for our men and women in uniform, it is just another day that carves out our sacrifice in minutes, hours, seconds; bravery, diversity and courage. Unless you have worn the cloth of our nation – you do not understand our sacrifice, nor do we ask that of you. We, represent the freedom by which you stand. We, are, the, light, in, the, flame, that, illuminates, our, great, lady, of, liberty. I am proud to be an American, wearing the cloth, which keeps our country free.

"Well great Americans, thanks for another wonderful day." I've heard those words daily since June 2003 – I've talked to the man who says them, but I've never seen his face, even when standing in the same room as him. Freedom – it isn't free.

I am gone. As your eyes dance across the bits and bytes that have been re-assembled on the screen before you, I am defying life in a different way – I am flying across the world to my new home.

Fair Winds and Following Seas --- Paul

I landed back in America in December of 2003 and was greeted by my close friends Will and Diane. The three of us moved my things into my new condo in downtown Baltimore.

PART THREE

GREATEST SOURCE OF POWER

I was at a Groundhog Day party in 2011 when a woman asked me what church I attended. I told her that my partner and I were looking for a church and asked her where she attended. For the briefest of seconds I saw that flash of fear rush into her eyes as she asked me to clarify what I meant by partner. I told her that I have a male partner and pointed him out to her as we stood together munching crackers and drinking wine. Without missing a beat she said, and I quote, "I'm sorry, but your types aren't welcome in our church." My type . . . by that did she mean a retired military officer, a physician who saves lives or a committed couple in a loving relationship? The paradox of that moment was not lost on me; standing in a room full of people talking to a proclaimed Christian woman who had just judged my lifestyle and told me that in her eyes my sins were greater than hers. In that second it looked to me like she had just committed the sin of judgment, but instead of judging her openly I kept quiet.

According to the word of God, we are taught to accept one another just as Christ accepted us (Romans 15:7). As I stood with this woman I wondered if she truly knew the impact and meaning of her statement. I wondered aloud to her how a Christian church could reject anyone; for the purpose of a church is to welcome everyone and teach them the word according to God. Without missing a beat, she told me that her pastor didn't welcome same-sex couples into their church for he believes that their lifestyle is a sin. I wanted to ask her if she had ever sinned and what her pastor thought about his sins, but I pressed my tongue to the roof of my mouth instead. I could have reeled her into a longer discussion but instead I took the hook out of her mouth and let her swim back into the currents of Christian misunderstanding.

When I think about that verbal exchange I no longer get angry or worked up, instead I feel a sense of sadness for the misguided perceptions of what it means to be a Christian and what it means to be a homosexual.

If we are all sinners why is it that churches judge the purported sin of homosexuality with more zeal than the others? In that moment I wondered if she's ever struggled to be accepted in society, struggled with an issue that she cannot change or made any attempt to learn about what it actually means to love a person of the same sex. In her defense, I don't suppose the gay pride parades do us any favors as the celebrations do look a bit extreme, even to an older gay man like me. I, however, understand that the display of color and behavior is a reflection of frustration, pent up emotion and a single day where we cannot be stopped from coming together as a group of people to celebrate. It's an active display of unleashed carbonation onto the world, and for those cluck-clucking Christians right into their judgmental living rooms. I must admit, although I haven't actively participated in a gay pride parade for over 20+ years, I do smile at the courage and the cause that it represents . . . oh yes, and the overt display of emotion.

As we round the corner towards the end of my story, I wonder if you still believe that homosexuality is a choice. Do you believe that reparative therapy is an option? Is it possible to live a life where sexual expression is a part of our beings and not experience sex? Do you believe that homosexuals truly choose to live a life such as mine? What about the sin factor? I wonder . . .

You see, the greatest sources of power in my life have been my childhood, my walk with God and my personal discovery of what it means to be homosexual. The irony of all three is that I didn't have a choice in any of them. I was born into my family, God chose me to be His son and I was born gay. I wouldn't normally say I'm a slow learner, but it took me 40+ years to understand myself and accept the family dynamics that shaped me, the atonement of the Lord and the fact that I could not and cannot change my sexual nature.

Life has shown me that we can either be victims of our past or push onward to accept the authentic person who lives inside each one of us. It was only when I stopped struggling and accepted myself — truly accepted my authentic self — did my life change from confusion to clarity. Clarity came in Baltimore, so let's get back to the story.

MARK

(Age 35 - 40)

My Baltimore condo was in the heart of Mount Vernon on Saint Paul Street, just a few blocks from the local gay bars. Without intending, God and gay were now mixed together within my personal life and I was living on the street of a saint with a view of all the happy action from above. From a windowless tent in Doha Qatar to a home with windows in every room, I painted my condo with wild abandon; dark green for the bedroom, baby blue for the bathroom, burnt orange for the guest bedroom and a deep yellow for the living room. Although I hadn't managed to capture every color of the rainbow, there was no doubt that I was showing my colors to every guest who graced my doorstep.

My military co-workers had never graced my doorstep in the sixteen years I had served on active duty. I never wanted to have to explain my home life to anyone, but all of that changed when I went to work in Maryland. Charged with managing a large sum of money at a headquarters level, I was afforded the opportunity to work within my passion of financial management while teaming with two of the best men I'd ever worked alongside — Javier and Sean. Together we made a dynamic team for the Admiral who employed us.

I took a leap of faith when Sean invited me to an outdoor concert with his wife Cindy. He told me I could bring a date as long as I brought a blanket and some food. Unsure of how to proceed, I decided I would bring a "friend" and just let the evening unfold. I knew Sean couldn't ask me, and I couldn't tell him anything, so I decided to put the "Don't Ask, Don't Tell" policy to work. Nervous but unafraid, I showed up with my male date, who I said was a friend, and Sean and Cindy stood up to greet him and then we all sat down and socialized. Sean never asked, and I never told, but what I learned by the end of the evening was that Sean could have cared less who I was dating as long as I could do my job.

Javier, my boss, was of the same mindset as Sean. Although Javier was two ranks senior to me, he wasn't about to let me get out of social events after work. Greek food, beer at some local pubs, and Mexican food near the airport, he was always nudging and prodding me to come along and never questioned my relationship with the person I brought. Javier was more focused on making sure we worked together as a team and he understood that in order to make that happen we had to develop a rapport outside of work, which in turn encouraged teamwork on the job. Javier didn't care who I slept with either as long as I delivered during the day.

Feeling free from the burdens of my past, I slowly began to reconcile my walk with God and homosexuality. I knew I had attempted to change my sexual orientation through reparative therapy; I was divorced with a child, and although the religious chatter on television condemned my lifestyle as a "choice" and a sin, my heart told me differently. After so many years of struggling with this issue, my life's work had taught me it was not possible to change my sexual orientation, it was not a choice, and for the very first time in my life I came to terms with my truth –- the truth that God made me in His image as a gay man who is loved by Christ. Albert Einstein once said that insanity is doing the same thing over and over again and expecting different results, and I was now ready to change the equation. From a sinner to a man who truly felt born again, I was convinced that I was born a homosexual, and that is exactly what God intended. A bold statement, I know, and it took me 20+ years to discover this truth and just a few more to stop apologizing for it. Baltimore is where I threw the old framework of how I understood my life out of my twelfth floor window and began to live a life of freedom.

Like an underground network of captive slaves, the military also had a broad network of "closeted" gay men and women from all different rank structures –- enlisted to officer. There was an unspoken bond between all of us, and we made sure to look out for one another if the opportunity arose. I had that opportunity when one of the gay men I served with in Spain asked me if he could crash at my house for a few weeks while he readied himself to move across the country. I can't quite remember how we came to understand our sexual sameness, but I suppose it was like most encounters with other gay men, you just know. Although he was an enlisted man of senior rank, once the door closed on my apartment we were equals in every regard. Jared, that's his name, and he was the man who introduced me to Mark.

Two days before Thanksgiving I wanted to go to bed and Jared, true to form, wanted to go out. Back and forth like a seesaw, I finally gave in and let him push me off of my perch and out into the cold snowy night. Baltimore in the winter is similar to Saudi Arabia in the summer, shockingly drastic and no matter how prepared you are it always causes you to suck in your breath. One block over and two blocks down, we pushed open the door of a local gay bar and shucked our coats into the safety of the backroom. Not quite as shy as in my past, I had learned to smile and say hello to men as I felt them eye me up and down like a swirl of cotton candy at the fair. Now instead of melting from the heat of their stares, I had learned to puff my chest out a bit and walk on with a smile.

A few feet in and I smiled at a guy who looked like he could have been my brother, except that he had brown hair, brown eyes and chubbier cheeks. Definitely cute. Jared and I rounded the corner and then I stopped to sneak another peak at him. As soon as my eyes caught up with my arms and I saw him again, he was kissing the bartender on the mouth. It wasn't an open-mouth kiss, but it was a kiss nonetheless. Public displays of affection still made me squirm — even in a gay bar -- so I reluctantly crossed him off my mental list as way too openly gay for me to consider dating even though he was really good looking and had big brown eyes and nice hands and looked to be in shape and maybe had a decent career but I still wasn't sure about that kiss, so I moved on.

The next night, Jared pushed me out the door again around 10 p.m., claiming it was the busiest day of the year and the best day to find a decent man to date. For the record, it was the day before Thanksgiving, and unbeknownst to me it's actually one of the busiest nights in gay bars. When you think about all of the men who are dressed up for their family dinners and counting down the minutes so that they can escape from questions like "who are you dating" to go be with men that they want to date, a gay bar is a logical choice.

Back to the same spot as the previous night, and wouldn't you know, the guy I saw kissing the bartender was seated at the upstairs bar talking to a few other guys. I pointed him out to Jared and then asked the bartender who he was. I was told he was a physician, just got out of a relationship and single. At the word physician I counted him all but out.

Kissing in public and now a physician, I was disappointed for the second night in a row.

I had a gay friend who was a physician in Monterey, and while he was a great guy, he was the most self-absorbed, egotistical, maniacal man I had ever met. I had been through enough turbulence over the past ten years for ten people, and I wasn't going to get mixed up with a physician. Due to the fact that doctors spend most of their adult lives in school and then residency, I seriously doubted that self-actualized doctors exist; at least that's what I told myself. When the bartender sent a drink my way and told me it was from this guy Mark I smiled and waved. Mark did the same as the bartender sent him a drink and said it was from me. Smiles, a few waves, Jared nudging me in the ribs to go over and talk to him while I remained firmly planted on my barstool. Within a few minutes, Mark walked over — for the record he rubbed my leg — and said hello.

Handsome. That's what I had to say. He said he was shy as we got to talking and he reached out to brush his hand against mine. A few questions, several quiet exchanges, interjections from Jared and a lot of laughter, within an hour Mark asked me to dinner. He tried to give me his home phone number but I batted it away, giving him mine instead. I told him that if he wanted a date, he would have to call me and set it up. Although I had been back in America for just over one year, the tough outer shell of armor I secured to my body while living in Saudi Arabia was still falling off of my body, and I didn't suffer fools or foolishness lightly. If this guy wanted to go on a date he would have to call me. The next morning -- Thanksgiving Day -- Jared and I got on the train to New York City. We spent three glorious nights there, and I spent quite a bit of time taking Mark's phone calls.

There's something rather magical about dating around the holidays. Sparkling lights, snow-filled streets and colorful scarves wrapped around everyone's neck, Mark and I headed to dinner at the Owl Bar on a snowy evening; our first date. Our connection almost didn't come to fruition as he was ten minutes late — something about not being able to find parking — and with my water glass sweating, I was getting ready to leave. We spent the next three hours talking, and when he walked me to my condo I knew I wanted a second date and quite possibly a third.

Slow and steady, Mark was unlike any man I had ever met and held my attention in his soft firm hands. He was indeed shy outside of the gay bar, very quiet, humble and he had a curiosity about things I hadn't ever considered. On one of our dates when we went to watch the Mount Vernon Christmas tree lighting, he brought his Labrador retriever and his camera and proceeded to walk with his dog through the crowd of people while taking pictures. I was content to sit on the park bench and people watch, but Mark was more interested in what he saw than what others were seeing. Mark saw the world in a way I had never seen before, and he was blissfully unaware of anyone else's view but his own. Not a selfish man, Mark was merely true to himself as he allowed his own interests to take the lead.

No cell phone, no television and a beat up Volkswagen Jetta that housed his dog and his massive music collection -- that was Mark. I found it maddening that I couldn't call him whenever I wanted but instead had to dial a pager number and wait for him to call me back. His dog traveled with him wherever he went, including work, and his Labrador had free roam in the hospital to ride the elevator, wag his tail at the patients and meander his way through conferences and family meetings as if he were the doctor on duty. A classic example of Mark's world — his dog was truly his best friend and it only made sense that they were together like two middle aged men traversing life's adventures.

Backgammon, Scrabble, movies, dinners and copious amounts of conversation, our first date turned into three months of dating with Mark and his dog staying in my condo night after night. He had ended a nine year relationship the summer before and although he had been looking to move out of his parent's house since his breakup, I don't think either one of us expected this turn of events. A naval officer and a physician, we made a great intellectual match, but the understanding of power and control well, that took a little bit longer.

It didn't take long for me to meet Mark's family. His family unit still intact, they presented themselves as a Catholic example of holiness in which all of the family friends were still married, socialized together and supported their children. I wasn't quite sure if I had mistakenly walked onto the "Leave It to Beaver" television set or if I had actually just met the ideal of what America believes is a normal family, but they welcomed me with open arms. It was clear to me that their children came first as I was told tales of Mark's private boys' school, college and residency at Johns Hopkins Hospital. Picture perfect; it was so different from the family I had grown up in; I was caught off guard when my Mark's father called my competency into question.

Because I was a self-made man who entered the military with no college and was preparing to retire at age forty with two master's degrees, the thought of discrimination due to my military service had never crossed my mind. Mark and I had crossed the threshold of our one year anniversary when the kerfuffle began. Plain and simple, Mark's father informed him that he didn't believe I was good enough for the family. Apparently he had no conception of what it meant to work at the National Security Agency with a Top Secret clearance, and although I had tried to explain my job in the most discrete manner possible, his father continued to call my personal integrity into question. I was flabbergasted.

I'm not sure if my reaction was to his father's comments or to the frustration that I felt building over the past 35+ years, but in the clearest terms possible I told his parents that I wasn't going to apologize for the person that I am. It was a turning point for Mark and me, as it was the first time that Mark stood up to his parents and told them that if they were asking him to choose between them and me, he chose me. Although painful and sobering, the confrontation brought us closer together. We started house hunting.

Living in a big city allowed me the anonymity that was required of a military man living with a same-sex partner. With my military social obligations pared down to the barest of bones, I was able to go to work and perform my job while keeping my personal life separate. On the occasions when I was forced to attend a dinner or a social event at night, I did so solo, claiming that my physician girlfriend had to work. While I didn't try to hide my personal and professional lives from our close friends, we kept a secret veil in place between work and social functions and I always maintained the decorum of a heterosexual male in uniform. I wasn't sure I was always believed, but I knew that they couldn't ask and I couldn't tell.

Between the authority that Mark and I wielded at work and the family dynamics that swirled between us, Mark and I sought counseling together to keep our relationship intact. A fiery couple, we made several visible mistakes as we showed our friends and family the growth spurts of our relationship. I don't suppose it was clear to anyone but the two of us that we were committed to making our commitment work. There was a steely bond between Mark and me that held us together during our formative years. I allowed him into my heart as he guided me with a soft hand and quiet nudge, while he did the same for me as I met his invitation with a military mindset and unwavering opinions. Together, he softened my sharp edges while I honed his dull ones and over time we learned to complement each other. To our counselor, Robin — our collective hat goes off to you. During those first few years, you enlightened us with your firm tones and understanding words. You saved our relationship through your gift of counsel. Thank you.

As I grew personally and Mark and I entered our fourth year together, the military seemed to fall out of step with the cadence of my personal life. I was offered a job in Australia which I brought home to the kitchen table for Mark to assess. If I accepted this assignment I would have been required to move overseas for three years — alone. The military did not recognize same-sex relationships, and there was no way that Mark could be sponsored as my spouse to live overseas. Although I was tired of switching pronouns between he and she, there was a part of me that wanted to continue my career. I had worked for twenty years within the military, I understood the structure, I had persevered through the enlisted ranks to a mid-grade officer rank and withstood a multi-year investigation. Conversation after conversation, we toyed with the idea of a long-distance relationship, Australia or retirement. It was a tough decision, a decision that led us to Montana.

RETIREMENT
(Ages 40 - 41)

When I was promoted to the rank of Lieutenant Commander, my mom flew out for the ceremony, Mark's mother came, Mark came and several of my friends came, one who served as my "beard" for my promotion. I introduced her to my boss and my staff as my girlfriend as Mark sat quietly in the audience with our mothers watching from afar. A farce, I could have said my girlfriend had to work but on the occasion of something as important as a promotion it's difficult to explain away the absence of a significant other that no-one has met but whom I had referenced, when asked, for the past few years. Kristine, who is a PhD, was kind enough to lend us her doctor title for the day — two lies in one that got the job done as I was promoted to the next rank.

That promotion was a moment in which I realized that until the military policy of Don't Ask, Don't Tell was changed, I would never be free to serve our country as an authentic person. My relationship with Mark was an important part of my life and he was such an integral part of so many aspects of my personal growth that I felt bad when I dishonored his presence at my ceremony, but I had no other choice. The military did not allow homosexuals to serve openly and so I remained closed mouth about his involvement in my life as I thanked everyone in the room publicly — everyone except Mark. The only highlight of my day was Mark's joy as he was granted access to walk the hallowed halls of one of the most secretive agencies within our country — the National Security Agency. It was a thrill for him to be able to see what lurked inside, if only at an unclassified level, and I felt proud to have him see me in my uniform amongst my peers and within my workplace.

Faced with a decision to either move to Australia or retire, Mark and I made the joint decision for me to retire. Even as I type those words there's a part of me that struggles with the decision that we made, but without military policies or laws to support us, we had no other choice. Upon making my decision I informed my chain of command who tried to talk me out of it, but I held firm in my conviction that life with Mark had become more important to me than continuing my career in the military. I admit, I was jealous of my heterosexual counterparts who could bring their husbands or wives with them to every corner of the globe while the military welcomed them with open arms in the form of visas, sponsorship, housing, etc., but that just wasn't my life's reality as a man loving another man.

As I readied myself to retire, I went to have one final conversation about a possible retirement ceremony. I met with a female Navy Captain who had also worked her way up from the lowest enlisted ranks to one of the highest officer ranks within our service. As we sat at her table she implored me to honor my twenty year career with a retirement ceremony. I knew that she spoke truth when she told me that my ceremony was an example for those junior to me, an opportunity for me to show them what was possible in uniform, but what I couldn't tell her was the conflict it was causing me personally. For one fateful second I attempted to explain my personal relationship and as I danced around the subject of having a male partner I saw the terror flash across her eyes, so I closed that box as quickly as I could and we stood up and shook hands. In 2008 the prospect of allowing gays to serve openly in the United States military was still a daydream. I found it baffling that countries like Israel, Canada and Britain had all made the leap towards equality, but America was still holding strong in its conviction that allowing homosexuals to serve would ruin morale and destroy unit cohesiveness. Ironically, I knew of many gay men and women on active duty who were typically the top performers within their units but since they couldn't tell, their examples of professionalism and stellar performance remained in the closet right along with their personal lives. Leaving the Captain's office, that singular moment, is when I knew I had made the right decision to retire.

I've purposefully avoided talking about my rank, my accomplishments, my military assignments and the nature of my work, all of which have taken center stage of my daily life but they clearly have not been the focus of my journey. While my military career wasn't easy, I am grateful I was able to achieve beyond what I thought possible while I worked to understand myself. I'm sure there are some of you who are secretly wondering if I really was a top performer while on active duty or was I one of those men who skated through my military assignments with my head up my ass. To put all doubts at rest, I joined the Navy as a seaman recruit and I retired as a Lieutenant Commander. I joined the Navy without one single college course and I finished my career with a Master of Science and a Master of Arts degree in two different specialties. As for my performance, I was awarded the Defense Meritorious Service Medal, Joint Service Commendation Medal, Navy and Marine Corps Commendation Medal (4), Navy and Marine Corps Achievement Medal (4), Meritorious Unit Commendation, Good Conduct Medal (2), Navy Expeditionary Medal, National Defense Service Medal (2), Global War on Terrorism Expeditionary Medal, Global War on Terrorism Service Medal, Sea Service Deployment Ribbon (2), Navy Arctic Service Ribbon, and the Navy and Marine Corps Overseas Service Ribbon (4). I retired with three years, ten months and three days of sea time and three years of documented foreign service.

With the decision to retire, I counted down my last few months with eager anticipation. Serving as a department head for the Naval Security Group activity in Fort Meade, I did everything I could to ensure that the sailors working for me were afforded every single opportunity to excel beyond what they thought possible. I suppose I wasn't the most popular officer in my Command, and I suppose I had a reputation of being a "hard-ass" and unforgiving when it came to performance, but in my military mind it was incumbent upon those working for me to achieve as much as possible and I never asked them to work harder than I was willing to work.

There's an unspoken measure of success within the military ranks and it comes in the form of junior sailors asking you to re-enlist them. I was fortunate enough to be asked to re-enlist many, many sailors and to this day I still receive correspondence from some of the sailors I worked the hardest, thanking me for the standards I attempted to employ. The life of a Naval Officer is filled with a myriad of choices, quite a few tough decisions and situations that textbooks don't teach. As I readied myself to leave, I made peace with my military past and became grateful for the struggles I endured.

In May of 2008, I pulled into the secure parking lot of the National Security Agency one last time. I remember walking the halls thinking that after this day, I would never walk them again. I had no desire to become a defense contractor or work as a government civilian beyond my first year of retirement as it would have been close to impossible to suddenly "come out of the closet" to everyone I knew while working alongside them in civilian clothes. A person's reputation is the most valued asset within the close-knit workforce of the Agency, and I didn't have the strength to bring my hidden secret out in the open within this conservative environment, forcing me to explain my personal life yet once again. The military policy of not allowing homosexuals to serve openly was a major hurdle for me in securing work once I walked out the door, and Mark was the only person with whom I could talk about this.

As I readied myself to depart, I walked outside and stood under the flag pole looking up at the big glass windows of the National Security Agency. So many memories of my service to our country came flooding back to me in that moment. Magical, mysterious and a career I was forbidden to discuss, I walked around the outdoor grounds admiring the sacrifice of service of those who worked there, and I then turned around and went inside to hand in my badge. As I made my way to my car, I ran into a sailor with whom I had served years before. He told me that he had just been accepted to Officer Candidate School. Without hesitation I took off my collar devices, the rank devices on my cap and I handed them all over to him. My journey was over and so I passed my batons of authority on to the next generation. With a handshake and one last salute, I walked to my car, opened the door, started the engine and put my head down and cried.

CIVILIAN LIFE
(Age 41)

Taking off a military uniform is a lot like coming out of the closet. I was scared, I was uncertain of my future and even though I had a lot of education to back up my work experience, I was unsure of myself in a new way. I was no longer bound by the rules that had shaped me for the past twenty-one years and like a child without guidance, I wasn't quite sure of the new protocol of my life.

There is no doubt that President Clinton's policy of Don't Ask, Don't Tell allowed me to become a Naval Officer through the reinstatement of my clearance, however, this policy served to cripple me in the long term. I had only known how to keep my same-sex relationship a secret, so when faced with the reality of having to answer questions about my spouse or significant other as I started my new civilian job, I stammered and stuttered like my old 1978 push-button Ford Fiesta. I had no idea if it was OK to talk about the fact that I loved a man, a man with whom I had been in a four-year relationship and with whom I owned a house, one dog and two cars. I knew I could speak the facts aloud, but I was unsure of back room politics and possible hidden discrimination. The military had woefully prepared me to be completely authentic in every aspect of myself and I believed Don't Ask, Don't Tell was the cause.

As the Catholic Pope spoke out against a homosexual lifestyle, I wondered how many of my new co-workers were practicing Catholics. As Senator Larry Craig continued to defend his supposed gay foot tapping antics in the Minneapolis airport, I wondered if the new guys at work, in the stall next to me, were focused on my feet. As gay establishments were shut down in China before the Olympic Games, I wondered if when my co-workers asked me to join them for happy hour - they were wondering if I wanted to go to a gay bar. Questions that had never crossed my mind suddenly came into view in the most unexpected ways. I had never been required to present myself as an authentic person to anyone in uniform, and faced with the fact that I was now a gay male, a civilian gay male, working in a job as a defense contractor where they stated they did not discriminate well, I actually found that hard to believe.

There's a moment in every gay person's life when they are asked by a work acquaintance about their marital status or who they are dating. It's a moment that has required every single gay person to make a choice, a choice between truth and a half-truth. Up until this point I didn't know of any other way but to tell a half-truth because the honest truth would have compromised my career. I never told the truth unless I was in an unknown city in a gay bar or I was in a situation where I was with a friend being introduced to a new person in their life and I knew that they could both be trusted. It was a game of probability that took me many years to master, and it's a mental game that every single gay person you know has played. For me, to openly admit that I was gay felt like an opportunity for others to judge me, and without my uniform in place to shield the judgment of others, I felt naked.

As I fumbled my way through the first two months of my new job, I told some people I was gay; I told others I was in a relationship and I told my boss that my partner was a female physician. At forty-one years old, I should have known better than to think that my half-truths wouldn't come back to bite me in the ass, but I didn't have the tools in place to approach this situation any differently. When people in the military asked me about my spouse or partner, I lied and told them that he was a she. I had been switching pronouns and denying my sexual orientation for so long that I didn't think I was actually calling my credibility into question until my boss called me into her office and asked me if there was anything I wanted to tell her. I wondered what the hell she was talking about as I had completed my first several tasks ahead of schedule and typed up a summary of my accomplishments and action items every Friday. Laughing, she sat back in her chair and asked me again and again, and then again.

I think I understood her question as she phrased it for me for the seventh time. Bright red and rather sheepish, I explained myself in the best way I knew how. She praised my work performance and spoke highly of my recent accomplishments and then she laid the velvet hammer down on her desk with the force of her authority and position. The lesson that she illustrated for me is that a lie, even a lie about a person's private life, causes a chip in an employee's credibility — no matter how uncomfortable it is to admit the truth. Tough to hear, I listened, apologized, and then told her the truth.

What I learned in that meeting was that no matter what anyone else believes about homosexuality, I needed to speak my truth without fear of retribution, especially in the workplace. She taught me that it was much easier for people to overcome their prejudice regarding same-sex relationships than it was for people to overcome a belief that a fellow employee is a liar. For the past twenty-one years I had done nothing but lie about my sexuality and I was starting my new life as the same old liar, and that wasn't something I could accept within myself.

Just like the day I walked away from homosexuality at the tender age of twenty-five, this was the day I determined I would walk straight into the embrace of my homosexual lifestyle and declare it to the world. I promised myself that if asked, I would tell and if judged I would do my damndest to be the best ambassador for homosexuals that I could be. That was the last day I allowed my sexual preference to be a stumbling block that I could trip over. I was officially gay to everyone who asked me, and proud as hell!

MOVING

Mark and I were in our bedroom in Baltimore as the "Today Show" started shouting about life in the Seychelles. I was still lying in bed wondering what it would feel like to be on the hot sandy beach with a margarita and a good book when Mark looked over at me and stated he was ready for a change. Retired for six months and stuck in the hellish world of having to change in and out of different clothes every day, missing my uniform like never before, I had no idea what he was talking about. Mark wanted to move — literally pack up the house and move. Dumbfounded I got out of bed and turned down the TV volume.

Besides his college days, Mark had never lived anywhere but Baltimore. Born and bred in Maryland, I never thought we would leave our home with our screened in porch, elephant ears that stood close to six feet tall and the one hundred tulips that sprang forth like a bouquet in the backyard. Mark was born with five green thumbs and had transformed the outside of our home into a garden paradise complete with a pond, fish and so many varieties of plants that we could have opened our own garden center. I was in charge of mowing the lawn and getting the mail, which was really the extent of my garden experience, no matter how much Mark begged me to join him in the yard. It wasn't that I didn't like gardening, but I hadn't ever lived anywhere long enough to appreciate the nuance of getting dirt under my fingernails and was much more comfortable painting the inside of the house and laying down base molding than playing in the dirt. One of us inside while the other was out, our chores were divided as neatly between us as our t-shirts and underwear, which I taught Mark to fold military style.

Within a few days, Mark came home and told me that there was a physician job available for him in Missoula, Montana. I thought he was joking as Missoula only has two hospitals and Mark works in a specialized area of medicine, so I ignored him and turned the vacuum cleaner back on.

"HEY!" he shouted and then I knew he meant business. On the computer screen before me the facts told the truth. There was indeed one position open in his specialty –– in my hometown of Missoula.

Within the week, Mark applied for the job as I sorted out my emotions of moving back home after close to twenty-three years. My mom and dad were still alive, I had one friend in Missoula, Aarron, and my past seemed far enough away from my present life to be able to contemplate the Wild West one more time without breaking out into hives. We had traveled to Montana at least five times since the day we met and Mark fell in love with its Big Sky, big mountains and the beauty of Glacier Park. As the news came back that he was a final candidate for an interview, we collectively made peace with the possibility that Montana might be our new home.

The hospital in Montana emailed Mark to set up his airline tickets and in the process wanted to know his wife's name. Montana and gay. The truth of having to live another lie about our lives suddenly rushed into our reality and confronted us. I knew Missoula was liberal, but I wasn't sure how liberal and with Mark serving as a physician in a town of 65,000+ people, it wouldn't take long for word to spread that the East Coast doctor was a homosexual. Together, we decided that we would be completely honest about our lifestyle and if that disqualified us from the process we would accept their answer. Jokingly he wrote back that his wife's name was Paul and we would be coming together or not at all. Two days later we had plane tickets in hand and before the month was out we were headed to Montana for Mark's job interview.

Gay relationships take work and the beginning of ours took more work than everyone around us thought possible. Two men with professional careers, neither one of us were willing to submit to the other, and especially not with a tone of authority. I was the one in charge, while Mark thought he was and Mark was in charge, while I thought I was. Vacuuming, dusting, laundry, grocery shopping, car repairs, and every single domestic chore that is typically split into gender roles was up for grabs as we grabbed the house keys to our new home. Having met in a bar that we still liked to visit if only to see who could walk the balance beam of sidewalk cracks after several glasses of Jim Beam, it wasn't a good place for us to visit together as the visual temptations were so very tempting no matter how pure a person's heart. Through trial and error, we learned that domesticity is defined by making a home your own, and nightlife is better served to the younger generation who can still fit into a Lycra shirt without any hint of a pot belly. I suppose society teaches that to our heterosexual counterparts as they marry and get ready for children, but for gay couples without a resounding base of societal support, we learned the lesson of domesticity slowly.

There is no such thing as a knight on a white horse in shining armor, no matter how much Mark tried to convince me that he was him. Lust happens first, like happens second, and love happens over many fights and misunderstandings that sew your hearts together. There were many times that we wanted to pack it in, call it quits and move on to someone else, but something held us together. After four years together, and even in the initial stages when anger was quicker than a laugh, I believed I knew Mark's heart and could see his intentions. I had never met a more loving, tender or patient man; a man who was confident enough in himself to allow me to spring free from the judgment traps of my past and blossom. I may have gotten lucky in meeting a handsome and smart man, but as we boarded the plane for Montana I remember giving thanks for my relationship and the knowledge that no matter what the circumstance, Mark would be by my side, walking every step in sync with mine.

There are moments in life when you know a decision is as right as rain, and sitting at dinner with the hospital administrative and medical staffs, our answer was clear. The woman that Mark was looking to replace in Montana had made plans to move to Baltimore and had unknowingly applied for Mark's job. A few weeks later, Mark was hired into her position in Montana and she was hired into Mark's position in Baltimore. With the housing market collapse in full swing, we sold our home in Baltimore within the first three months and before the snow flew in Montana, Mark and I were settled into a new home and he into a new job.

TRANSITIONS

I don't make a very good house husband, maid, chef or caretaker. It only took me three months in Montana to figure this out as Mark came through the door after a long day of taking care of sick patients and I melted down like a plastic container in the microwave. I pronounced with the tone of my old military self that I was sick and tired of cleaning, I wasn't going to cook and I didn't agree to move to Montana so I could just sit around the house all day. To say that our first six months were rough, well, that would be an understatement. I threw every bit of gratitude out with the Monday morning trash, which I hauled out from the garage in my white bathrobe and clogs for all of the neighbors to see.

Our neighbors across the street refused to talk to us because of our sexual orientation. I waved, I took them a gift basket, I tried to talk with them when we were both out doing yard work and I was always met with the same reaction -- silence. I suppose I should have gotten the hint when they turned their heads as they drove by, but I always thought they were looking at their garage door to make sure it was either open or closed. I have this terrible habit of closing the garage door, pulling down the street and then turning around to make sure I did in fact close the garage door. Mark thinks I'm partially obsessive compulsive, but I think that's just ridiculous. My mind is usually already down the road watching for potholes, which is what I wanted to dig right in our neighbors driveway once I found out they wouldn't talk to us because we are gay.

I don't want to give you the wrong impression here; Missoula is the most liberal city in Montana and aside from the sinless Christian woman who said we weren't welcome in her church and our old neighbors; we really haven't had any problems here. Well, there was the one incident when my old boss told me that she wouldn't have hired me if she had known I was gay. She also proclaimed to be a Christian woman who "prayed" money into our organization – while she passed judgment on the company employees. Faced with open discrimination, I employed my military mindset and worked harder than what was required to ensure my contributions made a lasting impression.

It only made sense that Mark and I chose one of the most conservative states in our union to settle down and continue our lives together. While Mark works away at the hospital, it looks like my work has shifted towards a cause I never considered--the cause of illuminating what it means to be a homosexual within the American landscape. Now don't get me wrong here, I'm not a flag waving kind of guy, just a guy who has enough life experience to know that who I sleep with shouldn't matter to you unless you're in bed with me, and our two dogs make sure there's no extra room for anyone else. I am a man who has served our country, who has walked through reparative therapy, who had enough faith to follow the word of God through a marriage and a divorce, and who has lived in enough places to know that my good works won't mean anything unless I speak a truth that has the possibility of helping change personal perspectives and quite possibly lives.

Mid-life, my progressive bifocals have put Father Time into focus for me as I wonder when death will knock on my door. It's not a new thought; it's just in sharper focus, as I've always grappled with the concept that my life is going to end someday. It hits me randomly, like when I'm in the grocery store and I see an older person pushing his or her cart as slow as a turtle. I wonder what their life story is, I wonder what they think of the world, and I usually have to hold myself back from asking them if they are scared to die. I want to know if they think they've made a difference in the world and just how quickly time did pass now that it's moving at breakneck speed. Other times I am reminded of my impending death when Mark comes home from work and tells me of a nameless patient who had a stroke, a car accident that left them paralyzed or a teenager who has terminal cancer. I wonder why I have been spared from such tragedy and think about how lucky, I truly am. In moments such as these I know my purpose and now, so do you. I want to be the person whose life was an example for others to emulate, and the person who imparted wisdom well ahead of his time. So, for those of you who believe that homosexuality is a sin, or are struggling with this question -- now's the time to pay attention.

When I accepted Christ into my life, as a gay Christian, I believed -- just like my heterosexual counterparts, that in the moment I accepted him, I was forgiven for all of my sins. It is my understanding that I was forgiven for all of my past sins, my present sins and my future sins. In that moment I believed that once saved, always saved. This has served as the basic premise of my understanding of salvation.

As I've grown in my walk with Christ my focus has shifted from sinner to salvation. One of my favorite authors, Dan Stone writes in his book The Rest of the Gospel -- "The trouble is that, as true as this is, having your sins forgiven doesn't tell anyone of us one thing about how to live the life. ….It's as if the day we receive Him by faith, Jesus says "Now you're saved. Good luck. I'll see you when you die and it will be wonderful." But in the here and now, just get out there and try as hard as you can to live a sin free life." For me that meant denying my homosexuality, going through reparative therapy, marrying a woman – and failing at every aspect of my "forgiven" life.

Although I knew that all of my sins were forgiven, I never took time to understand what that meant. Once I began writing this book I slowly realized that I am always going to fall short in my life, but the difference between my past and my present is that I have come to embody the fact that I am forgiven. I have an "A" in the class of life, and I'm never going to get an "F" – no matter what I do. If I am forgiven of all of my sins then I don't see a need to answer the question of sin – specifically the question of homosexuality – because the question of sin will never leave my human life. I now understand that I am only saved, by Christ, and that no matter what my circumstance, my life should be about sharing my testimony through His will.

The question of homosexuality and its' sinful nature is irrelevant. With God in me, I am perfect (Colossians 3:12, Colossian 2:10 and Colossians 1:22). I believe that His desire is to perform His work through me, and that can only be accomplished if I am a continual work in progress as a human, a man, a father, a partner, a friend and all of the other aspects of my life. I now live according to what I believe is His will in my life – and I do so forgiven of all of my sins. Is homosexuality a sin? Well, that's for someone else to talk about while I go about the business of sharing the word of Christ.

God aside, there's one other message I believe I need to communicate, a message for homosexual men who are living out their lives in heterosexual marriages. I know the dance of shoving your feelings into the closet so your spouse is protected, while you disappear into the ether. I under-stand the conflict of wanting to be true to yourself and holding on to your secret so hard that sometimes you feel like you are killing yourself through a thousand tiny sacrifices of your own desire. I also know the aggressive acts of random homosexual sex that leave you so ridden with fear of having caught the HIV virus that you have trouble looking into your wife's eyes. You see, I've been there, I understand the dance, and I want you to know that when you finally muster up the courage to get off the roller coaster ride you call your life, everything becomes possible once again.

Yes, I loved my wife and yes, we made love throughout our seven-year marriage, but it was never quite the same as when I made love to Mark for the first time. When I finally allowed myself to become authentic and accept every single part of who I am, I was able to connect the dots that have eluded me for so long. I understand the fear of touching that part of you, the part you have denied for so long, but from this side looking back I can honestly tell you I wouldn't live my life any other way than as an open homosexual.

As I think about my life and how it parallels the struggles of so many others, I can't help but wonder what kind of life we could all have it we just had the courage to live our life's purpose.

ROUNDING THE CORNER

As I sit here in the mountains of Montana once again my life is truly free. I am at peace with my parents, I am at peace with my past, and I have a resounding sense of peace within my interpersonal relationships. I've shed my military skin and although I'm officially retired, I suppose I won't ever be able to stop my overpowering desire to achieve and experience new heights.

As for my family, it's taken several years for my father to feel comfortable enough to speak openly about my homosexuality. I realize that the role he once played in my life is no longer the role he plays today. My father has become a champion of support in my relationship with Mark, and I often joke that if Mark and I ever broke up my father would support Mark more than he would support me. My father loves Mark beyond what he is able to express, and for that, I am grateful. My dad played a pivotal role in pushing me to become the man I am today, and he did the best job he could with how he understood his life. Everyone deserves the opportunity to evolve and re-evaluate the circumstances of their lives, and I'm grateful that my father is in a place where he can appreciate me beyond a "preference" or a societal label.

My mom never hesitated in her acceptance of my lifestyle. She and I had other issues to work through as we grew into adulthood together, but her acceptance of my homosexuality was never a stumbling block between us. My mom is the perfect definition of a good friend. She listens, she attempts to understand, she never passes judgment and she always calls before she comes over. There's something so magical about a mother's love, and I couldn't have asked for a better mom.

Although I still pray and sing in tongues, my prayer life has changed. I no longer feel any guilt about my homosexual lifestyle, nor do I question its righteousness in the eyes of God. Going to church, leading youth groups, participating in Bible studies and men's groups are a part of my past. I give my private time directly to God with a hope that he will utilize my journey to not only glorify Him, but to shine a light of understanding into the lives of others. Religious zealots and talking heads seem completely out of touch with how I understand Christ's manifestation in my life.

Does reparative therapy work? No, it does not. If I could change my homosexuality would I? No, I would not. While I understand the desire of reparative therapy counselors, I believe that reparative therapy introduces contradictions into people's lives that have the potential to tip them over the psychological edge. People cannot change their sexual orientation, period. Reparative therapy is sponsored by the religious right, and it's wrong. I do not recommend reparative therapy for anyone.

If I have saved the best for last, then I would have to say that a renewed relationship between my sister and I has been the most unexpected and welcome gift of my prose. She caught wind of my writing and had the courage to reach out one more time, and this time our connection feels different. We're like two war torn enemy soldiers who have each come to terms with our role in the battle and are ready to lay down arms so that we can listen to the other's position. It's a battle that started in childhood, ripped us in half, and shoved us out different doors with different dreams. Her phone call a few weeks back felt like a sip of ice cold water after a long desert walk.

I am creative, I am spiritual, I am alive in Christ – and yes, I am a homosexual.